STONEWORK

TECHNIQUES AND PROJECTS

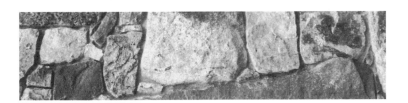

STONEWORK

TECHNIQUES AND PROJECTS

Charles McRaven

A Storey Publishing Book

Storey Communications, Inc.
Schoolhouse Road
Pownal, Vermont 05261

The mission of Storey Communications is to serve our customers by publishing practical information that encourages personal independence in harmony with the environment.

Edited by Elizabeth McHale and William Overstreet
Cover and text design by Mark Tomasi
Cover photograph by Steven Swinburne
Text production by Susan Bernier, Cindy McFarland, and Nat Stout
Photographs by Linda Moore McRaven and the author
Line drawings by Carl Fitzpatrick, except for those on page 38 by
    Douglas Merrilees, Ralph Scott, Chandis Ingenthron,
    Brigita Fuhrmann, and Alison Kolesar.
Indexed by Susan Olason

Printed in the United States by R.R. Donnelley

10 9 8 7 6 5 4 3 2 1

Library of Congress Cataloging-in-Publication Data

McRaven, Charles
    Stonework : techniques and projects / by Charles McRaven.
        p.   cm.
    Includes index.
    ISBN 0-88266-976-1   (pbk. : alk. paper)
        1. Building,   Stone.   I.   Title
    TH1201.M47   1997
    693' .—dc21   97-28290
                                                                        CIP

Contents

Acknowledgments

My professional life changed in 1978 with the publishing of my first nationally circulated book, *Building the Hewn Log House*. I transformed from a college professor having a minor obsession with stonemasonry, log house restoration, and writing, to a craftsman and preservationist having a major obsession with stonemasonry, log house restoration, and writing.

Without the help of many people, I could not continue to get my work published. Linda, my wife, partner, and photographer, who came to me from a world where getting things done — and doing them well — is an art in itself. Janet Pitt, my office commissar, who prepared the manuscript and brings things back to reality as often as I need it. Amanda, my eldest daughter, who thought dreaming about seeing Scotland would not substitute for *being there, doing that* — so she kidnapped me to share an adventure in the stone-strewn Highlands. Lauren, Chelsea, Ashley, and Charlie, my younger children, who pitched in with typing, photography, darkroom work, proofreading, and telling me when I am not "cool" enough.

I want to thank Cindy and Art Thiede, authors and photographers of *The Log Home Book*, for sharing their excellent photos (pages 43, 162, and 164) of our own house as well as of other projects we have built. Also, Tom Brody, my friend and founder of beautiful Endless Mountain Retreat Center, for his photos (pages 56, 92, 124, and 141) of the numerous stone projects built by both my crew and my students at his Bear Mountain Outdoor School, where I taught workshops for eight years.

Editor Elizabeth McHale for seeing new ideas in an old thought and for making me look at stonework with a different viewpoint from my first Storey/Garden Way book, *Building With Stone*.

I thank my readers for their many compliments and for inspiring this book.

Stonework is enduring.

■

Three sets of retaining walls hold back the mountainside for a house at Bear Mountain, Virginia.

Why Stone?

Why stone? Well, why not? For building or landscaping, you simply can't do better. Stone is weatherproof, ratproof, insect-proof, and long lived. Whether you use it in rustic or formal designs, it signifies good taste; a stone entryway, curving wall, arch, or path is quietly elegant and looks expensive.

In this age of throwaways, stone is also psychologically appealing; it represents strength, stability, and permanence. It provides a sense of shelter and security and blessed simplicity when we're tired of flimsiness and confusion.

A Tribute to Permanence

Placing one stone atop another goes back as far as our dimmest beginnings, and there's still something elemental in our use of stone in any form today. The art and craft of masonry involve a

This medieval Scottish fieldstone cottage shows the durability of stone as a building material.

Successive limestone defensive walls at York, England, show Roman, Norman, and medieval work. Little has changed since then — walls continue to be built the same way, using the same tools and the same mortar materials, and posing the same challenges.

kind of triumph over a hard, heavy, unyielding adversary. And once the rock is properly positioned, it's there, a monument for centuries. Stone cathedrals, medieval castles, and even ancient Roman arched bridges and aqueducts are still standing and will be around as long as anything we build today.

Of course, it's easier to work in concrete or acrylic-coated Styrofoam shapes. Wood, plastic, glass, steel, even brick and cinder block are easier to deal with than stones. You can injure your back if you don't handle them right. You can get chips in your eye, crush your foot, squash your finger, skin your shins, and experience incredible frustration when the stubborn things don't fit. But once stone is in place, it just *belongs*.

Building with stone is a tribute to permanence as well as a way of simply providing a dwelling for the future. It's not uncommon for European buildings to date from the Renaissance and before. At this writing, our eldest daughter is in Switzerland as an exchange student, living in an eight-hundred-year-old house. We can build for the ages, too, if we understand the material that is used.

The Philosophy of Stone

You're out on an abandoned, sunken road, cut deep a century ago by iron-shod wagon wheels. Tree branches meet overhead, forming a tunnel, with sunlight filtering through lacy leaves above. The road turns and climbs out across a hillside, spilling onto a built-up retaining wall of ancient stones below, with another dry-stacked wall to hold the hill above. The old shapes, almost completely covered with vines and moss, do their job of holding the road in quiet beauty. Contrast this with a modern roadway, carved from the hill, with bare concrete doing the same job. Romantic, isn't it?

Or you are strolling along an unpaved lane on an estate in rural Virginia. You find yourself surrounded by beautiful stone walls. To your right is an arc of curved stonework; to your left, a low retaining wall that gracefully descends at one end into a low bank of green. The bank gradually disappears as the lane approaches the main road, which is bordered on its other side by a long, straight, level, elegant, freestanding mortared wall. The three walls not only reflect, but also enhance, the value of the bucolic surroundings.

I guess it's a matter of philosophy — whether you want to speed along past concrete or move more leisurely past stone. Rushing is a choice, not a necessity. And that's what the use of stone is, really — a choice based on what it is, does, and calls to mind.

We have stone on the outside of much of our house, in one area stretching thirty feet up to the peak of the roof. We laid the

These retaining walls in central Virginia illustrate how well stonework blends with other materials, such as the brick used in this house, and how it adds value to a rural landscape.

stone between other jobs, when we had a few extra hours or days. It is not a cheap wall, but in terms of longevity and upkeep, it is not all that expensive, either. With today's mortar components, our stone should be in place five hundred years or so — longer, perhaps, if our successors keep a good roof on the house and don't let trees take root along its foundation.

No, it's not easy. We don't get trained naturally to do things the laborious way. And few of us will insist that our children learn how to lay stone or shape beams or construct shelter with simple tools. All of that requires work: learning how to do it, learning how to do it right. But there is great satisfaction in having laid unyielding stone well. You begin to hope that pride is a forgivable sin.

The Negative Side

Stone has a negative side, however. It's *heavy*. It requires footings that are stronger, deeper, and wider than those for other types of building. It sometimes requires elaborate lifting devices to get it up high enough for placement in walls, chimneys, and arches. Being heavy, it also is frequently dangerous to handle. Just as gravity and friction keep stone in place, they can make positioning it laborious and hazardous.

Stone is difficult to shape compared with wood and, of course, plastic substances, such as wet concrete and the clay that will become brick or tile. Shaping stone is unforgiving

Many complex structural innovations go back centuries. The stonework in these buildings in Edinburgh, Scotland, feature arches to keep the weight off the lintels over the windows (left of the center tower), and corbeling, which allows the tower's turret to cantilever out from the wall.

In this stone-veneered house built by Greg Quinn, arches over doors and windows constitute a handsome, functional design element.

work and the opposite of instant gratification. You pound away with hammer and chisel to trim an eighteen-inch stone for a seventeen-inch space, chipping insignificant bits, rounding the edges — and the whole thing breaks in the middle. Then you must start over. There are two solutions to this dilemma: Search long and hard for a stone that fits the space, or learn how to shape the material. Both take lots of time. And material. You need about three times as many stones to choose from as you'll actually use. (You'll probably want to start another project with the leftovers.)

Stone is a poor insulator; heat flows right through it. While our ancestors built with stone for permanence and tightness, we forget that they didn't heat their houses. They stood in front of the stone fireplace to get warm, and they dressed for the cold, outside and in. Water often froze in basins inside their homes during winter, whether the dwellings were of stone or not. A stone house needs some insulation to stop heat loss and a vapor barrier to keep the stone mass from sweating in temperature changes. Condensed water actually runs down the wall in many solid stone houses — thus, the popularity of stone veneering, which is about all most modern masons practice.

Stone takes a lot of time to lay, no doubt about it. A good mason can lay about twenty square feet a day *with* a helper. Some do thirty or more, but good, tight, artistic work takes time. And hunting for the right stone can take more time than shaping it. I do some shaping on about a third of the stones I lay, maybe only to knock off a corner or cut down a ridge. (I don't shape faces; I prefer aged surfaces to newly cut work.)

Time goes by as you select, fit, reject, shape, mortar, set, trim, and rake joints. I don't expect a beginning mason to lay

Master stonemason Dan Smith veneers a concrete block wall with stone to create a superior wall.

more than half a dozen square feet a day, but I insist that it be good work. Stonework is too permanent to leave in mistakes. One old mason kept referring to "be-holes" in fast, sloppy work. I had to ask.

"If you don't fill 'em, they'll *be* there," he explained, grinning.

If you do the stonework yourself and don't count the time, you can take as long as you want. But if you're paying a mason twenty dollars per hour plus ten dollars overhead plus some 20 percent or so profit to the contractor, you want to see some square footage going up. Time being money, many masons and customers like a flat, per-square-foot charge (from fifteen dollars to thirty-five dollars in central Virginia in 1997). But much of the satisfaction in stonework comes from doing it yourself. You can achieve that as well as an expensive-looking job for a reasonable amount of money. It just won't happen fast.

Take a 4-foot stone wall 50 feet long and 2 feet thick. After you've dug the ditch and poured the footing, there'll be 200 square feet per side, plus 100 square feet of top surface, plus 16 more for the ends. That's 516 square feet at, say, 5 square feet a day for you, the beginner, which comes to, maybe, 103 Saturdays. Two years. That's exactly half the reason more people don't do stone projects. (The other half is the hard work.) Now, if I laid that wall, I'd want 20 to 26 days, which at 5 workdays a week (no rain) would still take me 5 weeks.

So you get the picture: Stone requires time. Of course, that wall will be there for centuries, or until the new freeway comes through, but you'll have to invest time and muscle for that permanence.

Value and Craftsmanship

We've talked about some of the disadvantages of stone, but here's another major advantage. Suppose you stone veneer the exterior of a 2,000-square-foot house, maybe a 40-by-50-foot rectangle (ugly shape; let's give it some interesting angles, length). At 10 feet in height including foundation, that would be about 1,300 square feet of stone (with windows and doors out). At $30 per square foot, that's $39,000 for what amounts to exterior siding — maybe $25,000 more than what something else would cost. But the whole aspect of the house changes when it's built of stone. Your house will be worth at least $100,000 to $150,000 more because of the stone: That's value.

Stone becomes the focal point in any application. Stone quoins around a doorway or at the corners of a stucco house give the impression that the entire place is of stone. A shed with a stone front wall that I built in the Ozark Mountains has

This home in Edinburgh, Scotland, dates from 1630. Note the use of quoins, which ensure strong corners and openings for doors and windows.

A modern use of quoins on the McRaven house turns the corner from a stone wall to stucco.

always been referred to as stone, although it's mostly wood. The arched stone porch supports on our Virginia house are minimal, but they tie in with the other stone on the house and give the porch a sturdy, massive look.

Since stone walls were often whitewashed or stuccoed, you can get this look by using just a few stones, one here and there on a wall or chimney, surrounded by stucco. We once built a concrete block chimney for a client on a strict budget. We used a single stone in place of a block in several places on the chimney, and troweled masonry mortar over the rest of the block. To this day it looks like some of the mortar has broken away to show the real stone underneath.

But stone isn't stone isn't stone. Too many people don't know good stonework from bad and will pay for poor work.

We built a 4,200-square-foot house in a very expensive area ten years ago, and used probably 120 tons of stone in it. A woman who worked for the man who bought it, seeing our stonework, told me about having grown up in a stone house her father had built many years earlier. She planned to build one soon, she said, and would contact us.

She didn't get in touch with us, but a former carpenter of mine, bidding on her cabinetry, told me she was having the house built nearby. I called her and she asked us to bid on the stonework. Our bid was far too high, she informed us, and soon afterward she hired another contractor, one whose masons were notable for their sloppiness and low prices. This woman is now the very proud owner of a partially stone-veneered house that I must pass often. It is distinguished by probably the ugliest stonework in the region. It looks as if someone built a soft mortar wall, then threw chunks of rock at

This stonework violates all the rules: Mortar joints are too wide — stones appear to be floating in a cement wall; some stones are too small and irregular; mortar has been smeared. The stones could not possibly stay in position without mortar "glue."

it at random. Or as my brother said of one of my early attempts: too much wall and not enough stone.

The same thing happened with another couple. The husband had taken a course in masonry from me, so he knew the difference, but they opted for a low-priced job rather than no stone at all. Now they compete for the worst-looking stonework around.

My wife noted many years ago a basic truth in craftsmanship: Everyone has the God-given right to do sloppy work. Nowhere does it say that any handcraft will automatically be of high quality. Just look closely at many of those delightful old stone houses you see featured in the magazines on decorating and living in the country, and you'll see some really bad stonework. Or talk to an owner of a poorly made stone house who has to have stones replaced regularly, has rain come through the walls and heat flow out into nature, and must deal with perpetual dampness.

Recognizing Good Work

If you're contemplating stonework in any form, you must learn to recognize good work. And insist on it, whether you're contracting it out or doing it yourself. My favorite aspect of stone building is knowing that my clients are driving home to an example of fine work. You must approach your house every day, and if it fits where it is and blends with its surroundings, this is an uplifting experience. If, on the other hand, the house and grounds are ugly or jarring, that helps spoil your day. Every day.

The maintenance-free stone wing of this large frame house is its most distinguishing feature. Mixed shades of stone were used for the more than two thousand square feet of stonework.

Properly used, stone can blend a house and its adjunct buildings with the site better than anything else. Stone belongs: Use it and your structure belongs. Even if your site has no stone or if there's no stone nearby, we have all seen so much natural stone in our lives that we subconsciously expect it, particularly out in the woods. Using it simply fulfills that expectation.

Too often, however, people use cut stone or freshly quarried stone in an area of mossy outcroppings. Or they will choose the wrong, nonnative stone, because they have seen it somewhere or picked it out of a magazine. Structural stone should match native stone; if none is native, it should be natural looking, or as unchanged as possible. Excessive shaping and smoothness, fresh cuts, geometric cuteness, wide mortar joints — all destroy this feeling. Stone should never look as if it were really plastic that has been glued on. Weathered fieldstone is always the most agreeable to see, because that's what you see in nature.

The same criteria apply to stone used as accents in landscaping. A block of cut stone in a garden might as well be Styrofoam. You want character: deep weathering, lichen, moss if possible, a shape that makes you want to touch it. A mossy, irregular piece of granite, a lichened sandstone, or an eroded limestone will appear to have been where it is for much of its millions of years of age. Even in formal gardens, the man-made symmetry must give the impression of age.

Put simply, in landscaping, stone should be used as if it were there first. A turn in a path around a stone implies that the path had to skirt the stone. A small stone wall partly screened by dense plantings causes you to think there's a massive ledge or outcropping there. Use stone as the basis and work around it.

Even a low, unmortared (drystone) wall, with plants as accent, makes a landscaping focal point.

Early builders tried to shape stone so that it would look like brick. Folks had a basic fear of nature and the wilderness and wanted everything they built to establish the sovereignty of man. So stone was worried into ashlar patterns, chipped and cut and smoothed to belie its origins. Later, when concrete became popular, it was shaped into fake stones, but that never really caught on. Ersatz stone, often dyed, for some reason, was recognized for what it was: a rip-off.

With the insight of such modern architects as Frank Lloyd Wright and Fay Jones, stone in its natural appearance came into favor as a building material and continues to enjoy high status today. We have learned all over again to use what is out there as it should be used. Of course, poor folks in the backwoods were using stone this way all along. Foundations and chimneys and retaining walls were still being built by stacking one stone atop another, keeping all the natural beauty intact, perhaps without the builders even being aware of it. The more "civilized" builders just had to rediscover good stonework.

But it doesn't always follow that an abundance of good stone will mean good work is being done. In the Ouachita Mountains of western Arkansas, log cabins were often constructed with mud-and-stick chimneys even though ideal ledge sandstone covered the ground. Not until settlers from the East and from Europe arrived did well-built stone chimneys begin to appear in quantity.

I've been asked to do jobs in southern Arizona, Idaho, and other western states where good stone abounds, but interest in it is only beginning. In contrast, here in central Virginia I have trouble finding enough of the right stone to work with. I saw quality stonework at the McKelligan Canyon Amphitheater in El Paso, Texas, recently. The stone was good, but other local work was rough, with mortar smeared all over. It turned out that the amphitheater mason was from North Carolina, where there's a great demand for experienced work. When I teach stonemasonry, I emphasize appreciation as much as the craft itself. If you know good work, you can insist on it. If you don't, you can't.

Chimney, basement, foundations, and drystone retaining walls of the restored Pleasant Sowell house at the Michie Tavern complex near Charlottesville, Virginia, reflect the enduring beauty of stone.

Appreciating Stone

Not everyone will be able to learn to do first-rate stonework. Some of my apprentices pick up the basic skills in a few days; others never do. One carpenter who wanted to learn stone worked with me for two years, and his last job was no better than his first. Stonework is not for everyone. But everyone can learn from handling stone: the discipline, the craft, the satisfaction that comes from artfully placing this substance. Even if you do not become a master mason, the rewards are still great. You are building for all time.

So if nothing else, I hope you will come to understand stonework and the uses of stone and to add the appreciation of this material to your life; to be able to answer the question "Why stone?" with an informed "Why not?"

A stone house near the Manassas, Virginia, Civil War battlefield shows excellent use of corner stones as well as single lintel stones over the doors and windows.

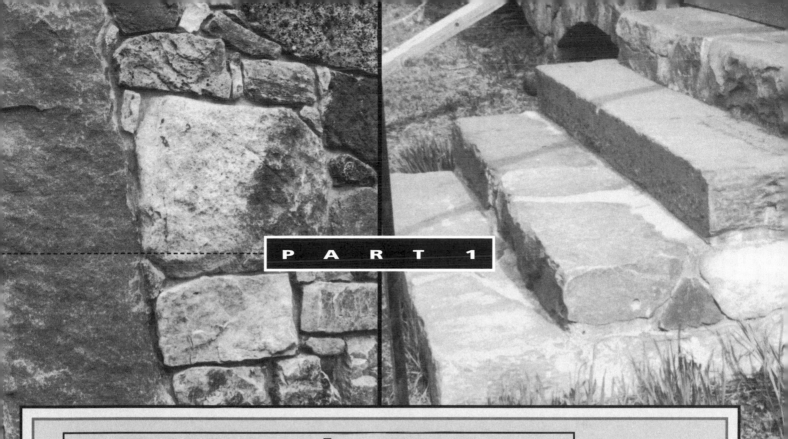

Working

WITH Stone

Built by various masons, these sample columns at a stoneyard feature assorted stone types and stone-laying styles.

CHAPTER 1

Types of Stone

BEFORE YOU LEARN how to build with stone, you should become famliar with some of the varieties you will encounter. You probably have heard of sedimentary, metamorphic, and igneous rocks, but you may not remember what these labels mean. From a building standpoint, they don't mean much, except in regard to workability and strength.

Sandstone and limestone are two of the most common sedimentary rocks. These are comparatively easy to shape and have less strength than the harder stones.

Igneous rocks, such as basalt and granite, are hard, less workable, and very strong. Basalt is volcanic, fine grained, and very dark in color. Granite, coarse grained and light colored, tends to weather and round off into spheres.

Metamorphic rocks, such as slate, gneiss, and schist, have been changed from their original state by heat and pressure. New minerals are formed by these processes. Slate, for example, was originally shale or clay. Gneiss is hard like granite but layered, characteristically in banded shades. It weathers along those layers but is hard to split. Most metamorphic rocks have a planar fabric or cleavage along which the rock tends to break most easily. This makes some metamorphic rock easy to work, as was the metamorphosed sandstone in the Pleasant Sowell house we moved and restored near Charlottesville, Virginia. Gray-green in color, it also contained small blue crystals. Workable yet strong, it retained some of the flat plane characteristics of sedimentary sandstone.

Sandstones and Quartzites

The most versatile building stones are the sandstones and quartzites. These range from coarse, soft, crumbly rocks to the dense, fine-grained creek quartzites that are so hard that they ring when struck.

Sandstones come in as many colors as does sand, sometimes rainbow combinations. In the Ozark Mountains near Clarksville, Arkansas, the sandstone is layered in an array of colors, which makes this a popular stone for veneer work. On the eastern slope of Shenandoah Mountain, bounding the Valley of Virginia, there is a purple-chocolate color that weathers gray. Prince Edward Island in Canada has a brick-red sandstone, which derives its color from hematite (iron oxide). All over the world are areas with grays, browns, whites, roses, and blues; the most common, though, are grays and browns.

Sandstone formed under pressure in lake bottoms has a definite grain, which means it is layered and can be easily split along the grain. It is best laid flat, the way it was formed. Set on edge, it may weather in such a way that the layers separate.

There's a great deal of difference between the soft, light gray sandstone from which I built my cabin chimney in southwest Missouri and, say, hard creek sandstone. I call a piece of worn quartzite that has survived tumbling in moving water a creekstone. It is dense and hard, or it would have come apart. Both types of stone are layered, but the creekstone is composed

This metamorphosed sandstone was used in the restoration of the Pleasant Sowell house at Michie Tavern in Virginia.

Worn sandstone slabs make good paths and patios, especially around pools.

of finer sand particles formed under greater pressure. Technically, these are really metamorphic rocks.

The sandstone you may have access to could be soft or hard, weak or strong. In mortared work, the stone should be at least as hard as the mortar. Of course, it will weather longer if it is hard, but the entire structure is only as strong as the mortar that holds it together.

Workability is important in masonry. If you have difficulty shaping any type of stone you use, the job is going to be harder. When you encounter stone that is new to you, experiment with it first by shaping a few pieces to get a feel for it. If your efforts produce only a few chips breaking off the corners, the stone may be too hard.

Any sandstone can be worked, but there's a logical limit. If you spend all your available time shaping, then efficiency plummets. Of course, you want to select well-shaped stones to begin with, thereby keeping shaping to a minimum.

Sandstone usually splits into even thicknesses in nature, so the critical top and bottom surfaces are already formed. Your shaping may be nothing more than a bit of nudging on the face of each stone to give an acceptable appearance.

Sandstone breaks naturally into pieces with flat tops and bottoms.

Squared limestone and sandstone have been used for centuries in commercial buildings, such as these in Edinburgh, Scotland.

Limestone

Limestone has always been a favorite building stone. Dense but not hard, it can be worked to almost any shape. Many commercial buildings were built of limestone, with the familiar chipped or bulged face. You can see these from Roman times up through the 1800s. Before concrete blocks (prior to around 1900), limestone — shaped and laid ashlar-pattern — was the accepted standard for commercial stonework.

Limestone is plentiful in the Shenandoah Valley, in West Virginia, Kentucky, much of Tennessee, and Missouri. It's generally dark gray, although in northern Kentucky it may take on a blue cast from the blue clay that is prevalent there. It can be almost black, weathering to near white as its surface ages.

Currently we are working with limestone chimneys and foundations from two log cabins in southwest Virginia. The roughly shaped stones, worked in the late 1700s and early 1800s, have weathered enough to support lichens and even some moss. Newly cut limestone has a slick surface that I find unattractive; weathered, top-of-the-ground limestone, on the other hand, often is rough, fissured, pockmarked, and interesting. Limestone may have fossil seashells in it, or trilobites and other traces of prehistoric life. Aging is a long process, but newly cut faces lose their fresh-cut look in five years or so.

Some limestone comes from inside cave surfaces and bears the shapes of small stalactites on it. Acids from decaying vegetation dissolve the stone, creating underground watercourses. These eventually collapse with surface weathering and erosion, leaving pieces with the built-up texture of the cave's solidified deposits.

Commercial quarrying of limestone, though greatly reduced, still goes on today. Crushed stone, riprap for holding slopes against erosion, and agricultural and mason's lime are products of the quarries. So are tombstones, which are usually of limestone, marble, or granite.

Laid as fieldstone, limestone looks natural and attractive. Now that there is so much synthetic stone in use, cut limestone surfaces have lost favor, and the fieldstone look is more popular. When laid as fieldstone, it's a good idea to avoid any fresh cuts on the exposed faces of the stones. It takes a few hundred years for them to age and blend with the rest.

riprap

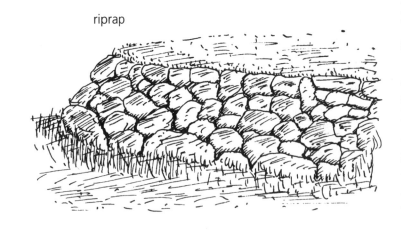

In drystone work — that is, stonework without mortar — both sandstone and limestone are ideal because of their evenly layered strata. The more bricklike in shape, the easier it is to lay drystone. And with the inevitable sprouting of plants from the crevices, these walls age well.

Granite and Greenstone

Granites are generally rough-textured stones that are not naturally layered. Sometimes they do break apart in roughly rectangular shapes, and this is what you want to look for. The rounded granite pieces of northern Michigan and New England are frustrating to work with because they are hard to shape.

Granites have texture that, when weathered, provides a welcome environment for lichens and mosses. Strong and hard granites vary in color. Along the East Coast the familiar light gray granite is plentiful. Formed principally of feldspar and quartz, it's a favored landscaping stone. There are also dark blue, dark gray, greenish, even pink granites. The bluish variety of granite found around here is referred to locally as blue mountain rock, usually a rueful label. It weathers gray on the surface, is hard to work, and always seems to occur in quantity where you don't want it. If you want to use granite, try to find stones with the desired shapes.

Unfortunately, most of the usable granite rocks in our area were gathered many generations ago. (Up on the mountaintops, there are still good building stones scattered around; no one can get vehicles up there to bring them down.)

Gray granite weathers deeply, encouraging lichens and making it ideal for landscape accent stones.

Consequently, we often recycle foundation, chimney, and basement granite. Along a creek ten miles north of us there are a lot of big chunks of granite ranging from five hundred pounds to a ton. These require handling with a hydraulic tractor bucket or boom truck, which is why they are still there. The owners have given me their blessing to remove them.

There is a particularly mean stone in this region of Virginia called greenstone. It's an igneous rock, very hard and virtually unshapable with any efficiency. Like granite, it can occasionally be found in usable shapes way up on mountain slopes. The local quarry blasts out this stone and crushes it for riprap and gravel. You can buy it as building stone, but it usually has few parallel surfaces. Once in a while the operation encounters a deposit that breaks out in rectangles, and these are easy to work with. Unfortunately, all the surfaces are fresh breaks and fairly sterile in appearance.

Greenstone also occurs on mountainsides in long shards that ring like metal when struck. A fireplace wall in the ski lodge at Wintergreen in the Blue Ridge Mountains is made of

This wall in the McRaven dining area features mixed stone types, textures, and shapes — including a family favorite, the "elephant rock" master mason Dan Smith used.

this stone, laid as it was found. Although attractive, it somehow reminds me of prehistoric bones.

Shale, Slate, and Other Stones

You can find shale and slate and other soft, layered stones in many locations, but they're not very good as building stones.

We've just finished stabilizing the chimneys on the Theodore Roosevelt hunting lodge in southern Albemarle County, Virginia. They're of local slate. We had to push the leaning chimneys back into plumb and work concrete footings under them. We repointed, raking out the old lime-and-sand mortar, and used a high-lime-content replacement for strength. The secret with soft stone and brick is to restore with a relatively soft mortar; otherwise, the stone or brick may break apart with temperature fluctuations. Though now plumb and in good repair, these chimneys could still be rocked in any direction. The soft, layered slate actually compressed a little, allowing some movement over a thirty-foot height.

Other odd stones, such as quartz, are hard to work with and rarely look natural. I once found a rectangular piece of quartz that had lichens on its face and used it in an arched fireplace opening. I'm quite sure the lichens are long since gone, and there's now a shiny, white stone among those sandstones forming the arch.

You can use any type of stone you find that suits your purpose. If you want closely shaped stones, choose sedimentary rocks. For texture and permanence, use igneous, but don't expect to shape them much.

Try mixing stones, too. This gives added texture to a wall and keeps it from fading visually into a blank mass. If you have a limited supply available, mixing types can be especially effective.

Common Characteristics of Stone

type	weight	workability	strength
soft sandstone	light	easy	low
dense sandstone	medium	medium	medium to high
limestone	heavy	medium to hard	medium to high
granite	heavy	hardest	high
slate	medium	easy	low
clay shale	medium	easy	low
basalt	heavy	medium to hard	medium to high

The variety offered by a stoneyard, such as this one in Ruckersville, Virginia, gives a stonemason a choice of color, texture, shape, and size he cannot get if he gathers stone by himself in the wild. This difference is in the cost: Stoneyard stone has a high price.

CHAPTER 2

Sources of Stone

BEFORE YOU CAN WORK with stone, you have to get the stuff. And where you get it depends a lot on where you happen to be. Since one of our criteria for good stone is that it be as local as possible, start looking close to home.

Especially when prospecting, look for usable shapes, such as a flat top and bottom, with any appearance you want for what will be the face. When you find some, there'll usually be more of the same, since stone tends to fracture naturally along the same lines in a given area.

If stone looks doubtful for laying, pass it up. Bring home only the very best, and you'll still have a lot of rejects. Every stone will fit somewhere, but not necessarily where and when you want it. It's not worth the added weight to haul a rock you won't use.

Quarried flagstone, as in this patio, is sold by the square foot at stoneyards.

This mortared stone wall ramp uses flat Pennsylvania sandstone capstones over random structural sandstone from the Shenandoah Valley.

Stoneyards

The obvious place to begin is the nearest stoneyard. Most mine local stone for riprap and crush it for roadway gravel. But they usually also import fieldstone and quarried stone for veneer, paths, patios, and solid stonework. Newly quarried stone is fresh and sterile and will look that way for many years. Fieldstone, which is found on top of the ground, will be weathered, often with lichens, and have a patina of age.

Our local stoneyard offers Shenandoah sandstone, limestone, and Pennsylvania sandstone in blocks; the Pennsylvania stone is also available in veneer thicknesses. The locally quarried stone is a greenstone, called Catoctin after the mountains in Maryland. This local stone will occasionally break into usable rectangles, but not often. It is used primarily for riprap, to keep slopes from washing away. We've successfully blended it in walls with the aged greenstone from the top of the ground and with the local gray granite. It costs, at this writing, $45 a ton at the quarry, and we're allowed to handpick it. Shenandoah sandstone is $90 a ton, but also requires handpicking because it is not gathered by masons, so there are lots of unusable shapes. Pennsylvania "weatherface," at $150 a ton, is hand selected and nearly all usable.

We built a lengthy stone wall using Shenandoah and handgathered sandstone that we found ourselves, and capped it with slabs of weatherface. These were all sandstone, medium hard, gray and brown — probably the most used and most desirable stone in the United States today. Sandstone is a good stone to learn on because it cuts well, occurs in layers, and is porous enough to age quickly after shaping.

We use mostly quarried and field limestone to match other work in restoration. For the 1700s log cabin we're currently restoring in the lower Shenandoah Valley, we're using the original rough-shaped limestone for foundation and chimney. Replacement stones will come from other chimneys, basements, and foundations in the area.

Sometimes replacements aren't easy to find. In 1985, at Ash Lawn, the home of President James Monroe, we were restoring a slave cabin with a cut-slate foundation and chimney. Slate tends to flake apart, so we needed spare stone. Dan Smith was working with me then, and he tracked down the original Slate Hill quarry that the stones had come from. The owner was a policeman who liked to target practice there. Dan collected stone while the owner blasted away in his quarry firing range. The replacements matched perfectly.

In Arkansas, you can find the ledge sandstone of the Ozarks. In Missouri, there is field limestone. There are granites along the East Coast and elsewhere and greenstone in Maryland and Virginia. In sum, your local stoneyard is a good place to start.

Fields and Byways

But what about those rocks lying on top of the ground out in the woods, along country roads, piled out of fields?

Certainly. That's where the quarries get their fieldstone. Go prospecting, but remember that the stone you find already belongs to someone; check with the landowners and get permission to obtain it.

I have a favorite source ten miles from home where a creek has cut off the end of a ridge. The man who owns the land has piled granite out of his pasture and garden for many years. For a ten-dollar bill, I get enough to fill a three-quarter-ton pickup. As the hill erodes, more stone turns up; as he plows his garden,

This impressive entryway for a Virginia estate uses local cut shale. Although not as physically difficult to lay as large stones, Virginia shale breaks away in thin pieces, requiring much rock to do the job.

Stone piles, like this one, gathered from fields, may contain good building stone.

still more comes up. It is deeply weathered, rough textured, ideal for the old look we work for in our stone jobs.

Another source for my own projects is National Forest land. A moderately priced permit from the local ranger station allows me to hand-gather stone from specified locations for noncommercial use. No machinery or vehicles are allowed off the roads, and I get a limited number of pickup loads per year.

Various acquaintances of mine own woodland that has good stone on it. One lets me take sandstone from her mountaintop for work done on her log cabin. Another lets me raid the piles that have grown from clearing fields along his creek bank.

Stonemason Eric Bolton restored this drystone-look mortared chimney, stone by numbered stone, for the Sowell house, which has won many awards for restoration excellence.

The Missing Quarry

My most intriguing search for stones came in 1993 in connection with the Sowell house restoration we did for Michie Tavern, near Thomas Jefferson's Monticello, outside Charlottesville, Virginia. The post-and-beam house was built around 1822 by a furniture and coffin maker named Pleasant Sowell. We dismantled the place piece by piece, charting, coding, and photographing floorboards, beams, and, of course, basement and chimney stones. There were 170 tons of a curious, greenish stone, hand drilled and quarried using stone feathers and wedges to crack and split it. Some stones weighed seven hundred pounds and were five feet long.

No stone like this existed near the site except for a slave cabin chimney and a fallen springhouse. Other outbuilding foundations were of the hard, mean, local greenstone. We searched the surrounding area but could not locate anything like it. If the original mason had hauled, say, a ton at a time with horse and wagon, he would have made 170 trips from somewhere. No commercial quarries were operating there in the 1820s, we discovered. Work was being done along rivers for navigation locks and dams, but this was miles away and the stone was different. Where did Sowell get his stone?

We never found out. The best guess is that there may have been a small nearby quarry to supply foundation stone for the redbrick buildings of architect Jefferson's University of Virginia. Perhaps our man had worked at the university, possibly hauling home quarried stone at the end of the day or week. That's at least six miles, probably more by the roads. Any such quarry is lost to records today, the site long since covered over.

My geologist friend Nick Evans identified the stone as metamorphosed sandstone and directed me to the next county, where I could find a similar but gray stone for replacements. It occurred next to the veins of soapstone that have been quarried for many years in Virginia. That stone, so workable, is among my favorites. If only I could just find more of it.

When I teach stonebuilding workshops at Bear Mountain School near Hightown in western Virginia, part of the course work involves gathering stone. Tom Brody, who runs the outdoor school, obtains permission from the landowners, and off the students go for hands-on gathering. We take pry bars along to turn up the stones, and several of us get together to lift the big ones. We treat it as an adventure. And it's excellent training in getting only the stone you can lay in place. After you've searched for just the right rock, you won't bring something home that you can't use.

Rock along roadsides is questionable. The best approach is to contact the adjoining landowner, even if the stone is in the road right-of-way; otherwise, you can make yourself unpopular by assuming that no one wants those stones. When we collect rock near roadways, we usually take two pickup trucks. That way we can double up on large stones and get about three tons a trip. One of my favorite sources is ninety-five miles away, so it's an all-day project. Sometimes we take a big flatbed truck, but it's too high a lift for large stones unless there are at least three of us. Each of us amasses piles along the roadway, then we load them together.

Mountains and Creeks

In mountainous country, you can often find good stones on the slopes and up on top where there are no roads. Problem is, how do you get them? One mason asked the excavator who had dug his basement to push a path up his mountain. It was very steep

---

Gathering Precautions

When out gathering stone, here are several precautions to take:

- Pay attention to the terrain. West and north of my central Virginia home, a number of steep mountain slopes have big rockslides with thousands of fine stones. They're always hard to get to, though, and pulling out the wrong rock can start an avalanche and bury you quickly.
- Be sure of your footing. It's easy to slip while carrying a stone, especially from a streambed. Falling is bad enough; with a hundred-pound stone on top of you, it's downright annoying.
- Tell people where you're going stone prospecting or, better, take another person with you (and *both* of you tell others).
- Keep a sharp eye out for snakes, wasps, and poison ivy.
- Don't be in a hurry around stone. That goes for transporting and laying as well as gathering. Stones are accustomed to waiting.

Riverbeds can be good sources for natural flagstone and building stone. Gathering at the source is daunting but not impossible.

for maneuvering, but the operator drove the track loader straight up and backed straight down with his hand-loaded bucket full.

I did that with native greenstone for the cabin John Kluge asked us to build in 1987. I had a John Deere wheel tractor with bucket, which I almost turned over more than once. Not only did I have to go straight up and back down, but I also had to drag the bucketful of stone on the ground to slow down. The tractor had brakes only on the back wheels, and with a bucketful up front, the wheels just slid. But coming down, forward would have been worse, so we mounted a big boulder on the three-point hitch to help hold down the back end.

On really steep slopes, we tumble the stones down, maybe a dozen at a time to a level place we can reach with a truck. There are some spectacular rockslides in the Blue Ridge and in the Virginia Appalachians, and sometimes you can work good stones down and not kill yourself.

For patio or pathway stone, we prospect creek beds. Frederica (Fred) Lashley, a mason in Asheville, North Carolina, has worked with us on stone projects. She uses a four-wheel-drive pickup to get into backcountry creeks for flat flagstone. Fred usually loads by hand but can rig slings and cables in minutes to lift big rocks. She and my daughter Amanda moved a large five-foot slab seventy-five feet with pry bars and a come-along — that is, a rachet hand winch — to a creek bank, then slid it into her truck. It took five of us to unload it.

Creekstones are usually smooth and rounded at the edge, which makes them ideal for patios around swimming pools, where people go barefoot. Ledge sandstone, on the other hand, can be rough and sharp edged. The little cabin my wife, Linda, and I built in Missouri had a flagstone floor of the thin-layered limestone from our spring creek. We installed heating cables under the floor, which was pleasantly warm to stand on in winter but cool in summer. Note, however, that not all creekstone has a rounded, smooth, tumbled texture; some will break off in slabs.

I particularly like creeks and riverbeds. After I've taken select stones, I can go back in six months and there will be more. The major drawback is that all the loading is uphill. I try to find a place where I can back the truck to the bank, then stack the stone up there from below for loading.

Recycled Stone

I like recycled stones and often stop to ask about abandoned chimneys where houses have burned. Sometimes these stones are free; sometimes they're not for sale at any price. I offer a basic ten dollars per pickup load or fifty dollars a flatbed load.

Most older structures were dry laid, with just clay between the stones. The stones had to be good to stay in place, so there's little waste. Be sure to handpick; if you scoop them up with a loader bucket, you get a lot of dirt and rubble and other unusable stuff.

Our house has a blue-gray stone we found in Lynchburg, Virginia, when old downtown buildings were being torn out a dozen years ago. For twenty-five dollars, the loader operator would pile about eight tons onto my flatbed truck. It had been quarried by hand about 150 years ago. We mixed it with Shenandoah Valley sandstone. This quarried stone is often too neat by itself, but mixed in with fieldstone, it can look just fine.

Dismantling a log cabin in West Virginia in 1984, we found a lot of basement and chimney stone with wide cut marks on it. The former owner told me that his grandfather and other local men had shoveled the soil off this soft sandstone and quarried it wet out of the ground. They'd used axes to work the soft stone, which dried hard. Much of it is now in our house.

If you elect to dismantle a structure for the stone — a chimney or basement or house wall, for example — check first to see how it is put together. Lime-and-sand mortar, used for centuries until around 1900, can be dug out easily and allows the stones to separate nicely. Modern Portland cement, however, forms a strong bond, makes it hard to get the stones apart, and is difficult to remove from the stones themselves. If the stones are cemented with Portland, you'll have a lot of chiseling to do, and the stains will stay on the stones. I seldom reuse chimney or wall stones if I have to grapple with modern cement.

A chimney is usually startlingly easy to pull over, with a long cable and a tractor or four-wheel-drive vehicle. You get the

Abandoned chimneys and foundations are often excellent sources for stone

Multicolored stones from various sources — some quarried, some fieldstone, some recycled — went into constructing the stairwell tower in the McRaven house.

chimney rocking and once it's really off-center, down it comes. Stones, dust, mortar fly everywhere, so stay at least a hundred feet away. When we plan to restore a unique chimney just as we find it, we number the stones and remove them by hand, using scaffolding. If the ground is soft, most stones can be dropped without damage, but in many cases we pass each one down hand to hand. This is always our method when we're dealing with a National Historic Register structure.

A wall laid with lime mortar can be pried apart easily with a crowbar, one stone at a time. Sometimes sections can be pulled down with a tractor, but a lot gets lost in the rubble. Wear a dust mask around this kind of work, and never demolish stonework in a stiff wind.

Friends and Other Sources

Stone sources are a matter of keeping your eyes open and pursuing leads. Sometimes, though, none of them pans out, such as the day I spent tracking down an available house basement (it turned out to be brick), several large piles of stone from plantation fields (none usable), and a chimney (the owner wouldn't sell). On other occasions, I've found half a dozen landowners who either gave me stone or charged only a token amount. One man even cut a special gateway in his pasture fence for me.

Many masons will gather stone from various places and sell to you in an off period. Naturally, they will want to keep the best for themselves, so insist on handpicking. Another source is leftovers from someone else's job. An offer to clean up the remaining stone from a building site, cheap, may get you some valuable material.

You can locate stone of a given type by visiting your state geology or mineral resource headquarters. Field geologists map stone underlayment and can tell you where certain stones occur. Once you've located them, contact the landowners in the areas chosen to make arrangements for obtaining the stone.

When you become aware of stone, you'll be surprised at how much is available. I cannot take a trip anywhere without checking out the stones I see. My usual transportation these days is a pickup truck, so I can load a few stones when I find them. I'll ask around first to locate landowners and get permission, then return with help later for serious quantities.

My old friend Bill Cameron collected stone on his travels as a mill-supply salesman during the Depression, hauling it home in the trunk of his car. Eventually he had enough to have a stone cottage built above Lake Taneycomo in Branson, Missouri.

Strange Ideas

People get odd notions.

A man from southern Arizona liked the look of Missouri limestone and wanted an elaborate house built of it, although there isn't any such stone near his site. He trucked tons of it halfway across the United States to build a house that must look completely out of place.

Recently, the builders of the new Tuacahn Amphitheater in St. George, Utah, wanted to use native red sandstone in the project. They actually found it cheaper to have the stone quarried, cut to specifications, and shipped — *from India*. It's a good match, but the logistics of it just don't make sense to me.

I have stones from all over, too. A Russian fireplace we're building in our house will have in it stone from Prince Edward Island and a fossil-filled sandstone block from West Virginia. Our house has a sandstone from my friend Ken Smith's place in Fayetteville, Arkansas, and the fireplace has a pair of pink granite cobblestones from Dublin that Bill Cameron gave us. There are fossil limestones from Missouri, recycled foundation stones from an old Virginia theater, white sandstone from a mountaintop that I'm told was once lake bottom in West Virginia, and soapstone from an old plantation house chimney.

I maintain a pile of stone — about ten tons — near my house. Since I have finally finished the exterior stone veneer, however, my wife has suggested repeatedly that I remove it. You might want to find a suitable place to store your stone, because you will not use it all up quickly. (My house-stone supply is fourteen years old.)

It's cheaper to find your own stone than to buy it at the quarry. It's more work, too, but it gives you an excuse to get out into the country. So lay a sheet of plywood in your pickup truck bed to protect it, and have fun prospecting.

This fossil-filled sandstone from a West Virginia mountaintop will be used in a long-planned project — a Russian fireplace in the McRaven house.

Lifting stones can be done by hand — with care, help, and proper scaffolding. Here, McRaven Restorations crewmen Don Crotteau and Jim Roepke build a chimney using recycled stone from a log house, with other stones mixed in to vary color, size, and texture.

CHAPTER 3

Handling Stone

EVEN IN THIS HIGH-TECH AGE, most stoneworkers still pick up, load, stack, select, shape, and place stone by hand. In a single day, a mason may handle ten tons of stone, one stone at a time, and many of the same stones several times.

For really big stones, which I characterize as those requiring more than two people to handle, my crew and I use machinery. That includes everything from a simple pry bar, block and tackle, or come-along (a hand-operated ratchet hoist) to an electric winch, a hydraulically activated boom mounted on a truck, a hydraulic jack, or a tractor with bucket. It depends on where you are and how much room you have to maneuver. Unlike big commercial construction sites with flat, uncluttered access, most stone-gathering and stone-laying sites are among trees, on sloping ground, or against walls, where there is little room.

Lifting and Loading Devices

Loading devices are many and ingenious. We recently winched several large stones (an average of four hundred pounds) up a creek bank with my Land Rover PTO winch, which runs off a shaft from the transmission, but we had no way to lift them onto the flatbed. Fred Lashley rigged a cable between two trees with nylon webbing, one end through a snatch block. She used a pull-through come-along and another snatch block on the trussed stone to double her lifting power. When she had each stone up, I backed the truck underneath, and she lowered it onto the bed.

This was in a sunken road where the trees grew close. Even if we'd had a tractor with loader bucket, we couldn't have maneuvered well. On this same trip, we skidded really big stones up heavy loading planks with the winch. I'd had my eye on a seven-foot stone that had broken off a ledge, about twelve inches square in section. We pulled it across the creek and, positioning the Rover beyond the flatbed at right angles, pulled it up much as you would load a log with skid poles. The stone will cap a drystone entry wall I'm building with really big stones that I've collected over several years.

You will seldom have heavy equipment out in the woods where you find stone, but you can rig a tripod, even if there are no trees handy. Make it tall, of doubled two-by-fours about twelve feet long. Wrap chain around the apex and hold it in place with some twenty-penny spikes. Hook a come-along into this chain and wrap another chain around the stone. Set the legs of this tripod far enough apart to allow your pickup truck to back between. Lift the stone, back under, and let it down. The process isn't fast, but this stone will cover more area than several smaller ones and will look better, too.

You can often pry or pull a big stone to the edge of a bank and get your truck below it. If you can't get right up to the bank, use heavy planks (I use two-by-twelve oak) to slide the stone onto the truck.

The angle-iron rack on my pickup is heavy enough (I've beefed up the sheet iron where it's mounted) to hook a come-along directly onto it. I can pull a three-hundred-pound stone up sloped planks right to the front.

This is slow. It's a lot faster for two of us to work together, loading two trucks. We ignore the stones that are too heavy for two people, or wait until we come back with machinery. Remember, you still have to get the big ones into place on whatever you're building; sometimes a stone is just too big.

Very often, especially when I use my National Forest permit, I must transport stones a long way to the truck. I try to locate stone uphill, so I can work several down at a time, tumbling and sliding them. When the rock is downhill or a long way off, you just have to allow a lot of time. A ton of stone, six inches thick, will loosely cover your six-by-eight, full-size pickup bed (tightly laid, about thirty-five square feet). If you've carried an average one-square-foot stone each time, you've made thirty-five trips per ton.

One of the simplest loading devices is a small swiveling crane that mounts in a corner of a pickup bed. It is raised by a simple hydraulic jack and will lift more weight than you should subject the average pickup to. You can block under the rear bumper and load large stones with this little crane, but watch the limits of mounting bolts and braces.

We've enlarged this basic piece of equipment by mounting a fourteen-foot swinging steel boom onto the rear of a three-quarter-ton pickup. It has outriggers that lock down into place

This seven-foot ledge sandstone and other big stones require care, skill, and often equipment, such as winches, to move them.

Slide or tumble heavy stones up a loading plank into a truck.

A strong pickup truck rack will anchor a come-along to pull large stones.

to stabilize the truck — a necessity whenever a boom or swinging crane is used to lift heavy loads: A big rock swinging around out of control can cause lots of damage. A simple cylinder and a hand-operated hydraulic pump lift the boom, which rides over the cab on a cradle.

We've loaded and unloaded fifteen-hundred-pound stones with this rig, being careful to tie onto the boom nearer the pivot point with the heavier loads. With the pivot seven feet high, we can theoretically set a stone about twenty feet up on a wall, chimney, or scaffold board, from where it can be hand-set. It would be much faster with a motor-driven hydraulic pump, lift and swivel control valves, and a hinged articulating boom, but it would also be more expensive.

Of Trucks and Loads

My two-wheel-drive, six-cylinder F-250 pickup truck is an ideal all-around construction vehicle. It doesn't have a heavy-duty differential, but I routinely carry a ton and a half of stone — two tons on short hauls. A heavier truck would use more fuel; a lighter one wouldn't haul much. With 260,000 miles on it, the pickup really doesn't owe me anything more, so it's almost free transportation. I may replace it eventually with a heavier, four-wheel-drive diesel, because there are many creek beds that I can't get into. Or if I get another cheaper two-wheel drive, I'll mount a winch on the front.

I've frequently used a two-wheel trailer pulled by my Land Rover for hauling stone, but it's harder to maneuver than a pickup. As I age, I increasingly appreciate things like power steering, better heaters, better visibility. I'll never retire my Rover, but I don't beat it up hauling stone anymore.

While we're on the subject of trucks, please heed this bit of advice. Don't get an automatic transmission if you plan to haul stone in hilly country. It's not much of a problem going uphill, but coming down is scary. The lowest gear just won't hold back a pickup loaded with stone on steep roads. My foreman, Eric Bolton, has a one-ton pickup with automatic transmission. We recently hauled two loads of stone from my friend's mountain in West Virginia, down a four-mile jeep trail of unrelenting pitch. Eric was never able to take his foot off the brake, and we had to stop three times to let the smoking linings cool down. With my four-speed, I let my truck idle down in first gear.

Another, worse story: While building a log-and-stone house at the ski resort near our home in Virginia, we had to scale a seven-mile mountain daily. One day a supply truck driver told us his clutch was slipping, and he was worried about getting back down. He didn't. Instead of getting the rig stopped safely and abandoning it, he tried to slow it enough to get all the way down. When his brakes failed, there was nothing but hairpin turns at free-wheeling speed. Neither he nor his passenger survived.

The time spent actually lifting a heavy object like a four-hundred-pound stone isn't the problem. Getting it into position, trussing the stone, hooking up chains — that's the time-consuming part. The actual lift might take three minutes by hand and only thirty seconds with a motorized pump, but that's not much time lost.

You don't *have* to use big stones at all, but the stonemason's adage that a small one takes just as long to lay as a big one is largely true. And big stones look good. Generally, your work will be just fine with maximum two-man rocks, which can easily be two-foot expanses, maybe six inches thick.

For heights like chimneys, though, you'll find it takes too long to climb up scaffolding with each stone. Here we use the

For lifting very heavy stones, a hand-operated hydraulic boom combines flexibility and economy.

boom or an electric winch to lift a container of stones or mortar. We have heavy wire cages from the junkyard — they once contained bottles or jugs — that we rig with lifting chains at three points for stability. The winch is a twelve-volt one that we bolt to a heavy scaffold walkboard for straight lifts. For chimney construction, we attach the scaffolding solidly to the house.

Where there's room, a tractor with bucket is helpful. You can hang a chain from the bucket to wrap around stones, or load them into the bucket. On sloping ground, however, beware of lifting the loaded bucket up high; the tractor can turn over in an instant. One of my worst moments came when I had backed my tractor around with a big stone swinging from the uplifted bucket. I stopped, but the stone didn't. As it reached the end of its swing, the uphill rear wheel of the tractor lifted. I had my hand on the hydraulic lever and was able to drop the bucket just in time to set the tractor back on all fours, but it was a close call.

One That Got Away

As heavy as stones are, it's a shame they can't be trained to move themselves.

A few years ago, we reconstructed a two-hundred-year-old barn at the Michie Tavern complex, near Charlottesville, Virginia. We had no road to the barn site, so we inched my tractor down a steep slope to level the site enough for the barn, then winched it back out.

The foundation was to be drystone, using the biggest stones we could handle. We used a mix of large gray granite, the local greenstone, and Shenandoah Valley sandstone. Our strategy was to haul the stones to a turnaround above the site, dump them, and tumble each stone down the steep drop, across a stream branch to the foundation.

We wired planks vertically around the tree trunks below to protect them, then dumped our first load. Some stones went down, but most stayed at the top, giving us a chance to slide them down with a measure of control. We tried cartwheeling some over the edge, but we never knew where these would end up.

I'd located the barn's corners and had built the near downhill one up about eighteen inches. We were moving more stones down when a flat one got away and began to cartwheel. It missed all the trees, jumped the stream, rolled up to the foundation, and actually hopped up onto the corner and lay flat. I wish I'd had a video camera. I suppose, given how many stones I've handled, that it was bound to happen. Trouble was, it wasn't the right rock for that corner.

The basement wall of this two-hundred-year-old barn at the Michie Tavern complex was restored without mortar. The barn is used for material storage.

As you work with stone, you'll come up with your own ingenious devices for getting stones into place. Several years ago my brother John and I set a big fireplace lintel stone, probably six hundred pounds, by ourselves. We set one end of a heavy, wide beam on the floor, with the other elevated in the fireplace itself, on a big wooden block with an extended hydraulic jack under the beam. We inched the stone up the beam with crowbars, then let the jack down to bed it on the mortared side piers of the fireplace.

One mason we worked with owned a ladder-lifting device driven by a small, air-cooled engine. It would slide a platform of stones, mortar, or whatever up a heavy ladder. A braking device would hold the platform in place for unloading.

In general, you can move small quantities of stone by hand in the time it takes to set up machinery. If you're in reasonable physical shape and don't overdo it, you can get by with a wheelbarrow and pickup truck. If you do a lot of work or want to handle big stones, you might want to consider the advantages of more equipment. Stonemasons are a lot like fishermen and mechanics, though — they collect all sorts of tools they rarely use. Unless you plan to do a great deal of stonework, don't bother investing in expensive machinery.

Tools

The wheelbarrow actually will be your handiest tool. You can lay it on its side, slide a big stone in, and stand the wheelbarrow up by yourself to move it. (You may, however, need help laying the stone when you get it where you want it.) On rocky or steep ground, load the wheelbarrow back near the handles. You'll lift more, but the wheel will go over obstacles better. With the weight on the wheel, you don't have a good way to push, and even a pebble can stop you.

To load a large stone, lay the wheelbarrow on its side, slide the stone in . . .

. . . and pull the wheelbarrow upright.

Essential Tools

In addition to a sturdy wheelbarrow, I've reduced my essential tool and equipment list to these:

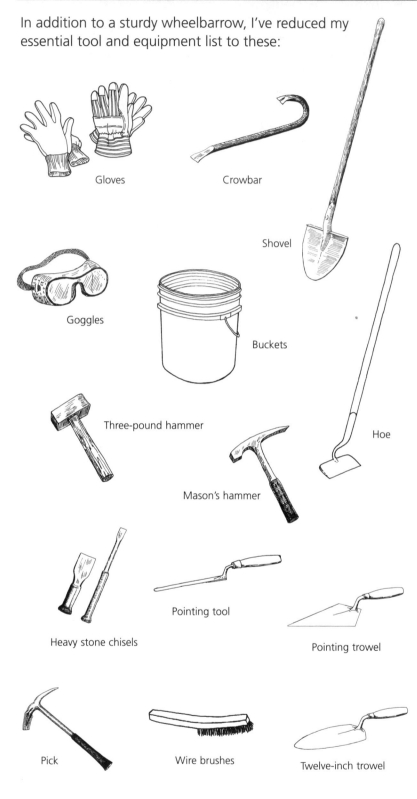

Gloves

Crowbar

Shovel

Goggles

Buckets

Three-pound hammer

Hoe

Mason's hammer

Heavy stone chisels

Pointing tool

Pointing trowel

Pick

Wire brushes

Twelve-inch trowel

When I'm working up high, I add scaffolding, a ladder, and an electric winch and lifting cage.

A hydraulic bucket on a tractor makes an efficient stone handler.

I forge my own chisels from automotive axle steel, although a seventy-five dollar carbide-tipped chisel works better. My problem is that things tend to get lost on jobs with lots of people around, and I'd rather lose one that took twenty minutes to forge than a good Bricknell chisel. Also, I like longer chisels, to keep some distance between my hand and the end that's struck. I make mine ten inches long, of one-inch or thicker steel. Axle-shaft steel has a medium carbon content and need only be quenched in water from a cherry red heat to harden. Higher carbon steel, such as big coil-spring steel, would require a separate process of tempering, or drawing the hardness after quenching, to reduce brittleness. I harden only two inches or so of the chisel's cutting edge and sharpen it to a ninety-degree angle. That reduces the likelihood of chipping, at both the cutting edge and the struck end. The struck end is allowed to normalize, or cool naturally. This way its steel composition allows it to be hit directly with the hammer.

My favorite hammer is a three-pound section of heavy, thick truck axle with a handle hole punched through from both sides. This makes a tapered hole both ways, which keeps the wedged handle tight. I like a thick handle for more control, so I make my own from shagbark hickory or ash.

I've made my own pointing tools, too, but prefer the flexible, wooden-handled ones by Marshalltown and by Goldblatt. Marshalltown also makes a wide but short trowel I like. By the end of the day, a long trowel is hard on your wrist.

Safety

I can't emphasize safety enough, when it comes to stonework. As a contractor, I pay a high rate for workers' compensation insurance to protect my employees doing dangerous work. Fortunately, we have few accidents, because I insist on safety precautions. A hard hat, goggles, gloves, steel-toed boots, and a dust mask are all necessities, as are scaffoldng for high work and a strong ladder.

The protection my workers like least is hard hats. But a couple of years ago, two of them had stretched a tarpaulin from the ground up to the top of a concrete basement wall we were veneering. To keep the plastic tarp in place, they'd set large stones on top of it. This kept the August sun off the stonework, and off the masons working under it. But the wind came up, and the flapping of the tarp began to tug at the weight stones. All at once, away went the tarp and down came the stones, right onto their hard hats.

Goggles are also a must around stone. If nothing else, there are always sand, chips, and dust blowing if any air is moving. And no matter how careful you are, a stone chip will eventually fly straight at your face. The worst injury I ever suffered occurred when a stray rock chip flew twelve feet and struck my eye from the side. The force of a hammer blow is transferred to velocity when that chip takes off. (True, goggles won't protect your earlobes, but you can see without them.)

Gloves help keep your hands from getting scratched, but not your fingers from getting smashed. (Your toes will be more fortunate, if you encase them in steel-toed boots.) Your hands do get rough without gloves, and in winter tend to crack, chap, and bleed no matter how much lotion you use. One helper put it nicely, though: "I wear gloves 'cause wife don't like my rough hands on her." Okay.

You may want to add a leather apron to your list of protective clothing. A leather apron will let you hold the stones close while lifting, without destroying your clothes. If it's long enough, the apron will also keep shins from getting scraped.

Use industrial-grade scaffolding in good condition for high work. The scaffolding must have extra-thick, wide, stable walkboards to work on. Stone puts an inordinate weight on this spidery structure. Know how to stabilize and secure the scaffolding to the building. The legs of the scaffolding must be put on solid footing, not on soft ground.

For construction in general, use a Grade I ladder. A Grade III household version is ridiculously flimsy, and Grade II isn't heavy enough either. The extra weight is worth it. Don't try working off a ladder — use scaffolding. The added weight of a stone you're handling can easily tip a ladder when you reach to work on or move a stone. Also, that weight can be all that's necessary to break a weak ladder rung.

Lifting Stones

With a substance as unforgiving as stone, it is hard to overemphasize the importance of lifting properly. Learn to *squat and lift with your legs.* If you can't do it that way, don't do it at all.

As I get older, I find I can't lift nearly as much with my legs. I resist the temptation to use my back, and just go for smaller stones. My ego isn't bruised a bit. A two-man rock just has to wait for another pair of hands. When in doubt, use heavy equipment to move and place stones.

For those stones you decide you can lift, the procedure is simple. Grab the stone in what would be a normal position, and then drop your rear another two feet. When lifting, hug the stone close. It's a lot easier on your back and arms, and besides, I suspect the stones like it.

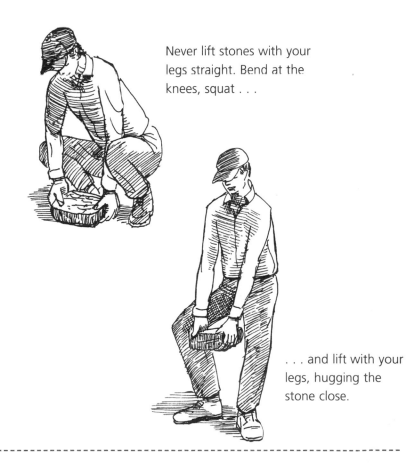

Never lift stones with your legs straight. Bend at the knees, squat . . .

. . . and lift with your legs, hugging the stone close.

Master stonemason Toru Oba built this exceptional veneer wall in Virginia. Such tight, difficult fits require good stone, skill in cutting, and true artistry.

CHAPTER 4

Selecting Stone for a Project

WHEN BUILDING WITH STONE, it isn't necessary to use all the same kind. In fact, too little variation in color and texture makes everything fade together. I go out of my way to mix colors, sizes, shapes, and surfaces so that each stone is distinct.

Several years ago, I hired a mason to do the chimney on a big house we were building. I'd bought a lot of my stone from him but mixed my work for the kind of texture I wanted. He did a great job but used gray sandstone without varying it. Up close you admire the workmanship; from a distance, though, that chimney loses its individuality as one stone blends with another.

Many tons of stone were used in the McRaven house. For the veneer stone, multi-shaded sandstone, six inches thick and flat-backed, was hand-picked during trips to the Blue Ridge and Allegheny Mountains.

Mixing Types and Colors

My own house has a collection of stone types. It's basically brown and gray sandstone from the upper Shenandoah but also includes blue-gray quarried stone flecked with mica from the James River area near Lynchburg, and lighter sandstone with brown iron stains from a West Virginia mountaintop. There's a deep brown-purple sandstone that occurs at certain levels near the West Virginia–Virginia line that weathers gray, and the local gray granite helps tie the house visually to outcroppings and buildings around it.

I got what I wanted, which was stonework that stands out. The joints are struck fairly deeply so that the mortar is in shadow. Big stones put it all into scale, since some of the work is thirty feet high. And even though a dozen of us worked on it over an eleven-year period, it hangs together because of the mixed stones.

Sandstone, one of my favorites, can be found in a variety of colors and textures. For example, there's the rainbow ledgestone from Arkansas and Tennessee. It occurs in narrow, horizontal layers that masons use freshly cut. The same stone will weather gray or brown, and many shades of each. Although here in central Virginia we don't have sandstone, we do have our pick of assorted granites, from the gray, deeply weathered variety consisting mostly of feldspar and quartz (also one of my favorites) to bluish and greenish granites. I'm told these are really schists and gneisses, but for masonry purposes they're granites.

The point is, various sandstones and granites can be mixed nicely together or with other stones. You can't shape the hard stuff very much, so you lay the others so that their shapes conform to it. And if you have had to bring in nonnative stone, this mixing can be the touch that ties the work to the site.

If you plan to mix stones, be sure to have a generous supply on hand. If you run out of a particular kind, the mix can get crazy from then on, so it's a good idea to ration your stones in order to keep the look you're working toward consistent. Mixing stones can, of course, help stretch a limited supply of one kind. In restoration work, we can't always duplicate the original stone exactly, so we blend in a mixture from the beginning, and it looks just fine.

Freshly cut stones don't blend well enough if they're very different in appearance. It's the patina, including the lichens, that lets a brown fit visually with a dark and a light gray. Even our greenstone looks good with the sandstone and granite if it is fieldstone, weathered by exposure.

We get requests to use flat, glue-on stones sometimes, but I resist that. A stone should look like it belongs, and no way does

Large stones above the mantel give this fireplace strength and an air of permanence.

a shiny, inch-thick rock set on edge look right. Ever. We've used flat ledge limestone with thicker blocks, but thin pieces on edge are not structurally sound, and soundness is a criterion for stonework.

Using Large Stones

Few things impart more of a sense of permanence than do large stones in a wall or other structure. First of all, they just *look* right, as if they grew there, or are part of a cliff or outcropping. Then the inevitable question arises: How did the mason get those big stones up there?

There's a way to place just about any stone you could want. But is it worth what it will cost in time and/or money to use a big rock? And, of course, you won't want just one. The whole business of artistry in stonework involves a creative balance, incorporating odd-shaped stones using verticals as an occasional accent, and emphasizing large stones without making them appear out of place.

Aside from aesthetics, there's an economic side to the use of big stones. Laying a six-square-foot stone takes a lot less time than laying six one-square-foot stones. Figure it will take you an hour per stone, whether it's large or small.

Before big stones can be laid, however, they must be gathered. And while it may be practical to rig a lifting device at the construction site, it's more difficult out in the woods. This is when the big flatbed truck comes in handy. The extra height is no problem with a boom, and we can get a large load in a day.

The truck also dumps, so unloading is reduced from hours to a few seconds.

My friend Cotton Coffey, a former student of mine at Bear Mountain Outdoor School, appreciates his big boom truck. He was driving through the mountains one day, returning from delivering a load of cabin logs, when he spied a nicely weathered, three-foot cube of granite he thought I'd like. In five minutes, he'd positioned his truck, slung the stone, and had it aboard. (I planned to put it in my entryway wall, but it's so weathered and so covered with lichens that now I'm considering using it outside instead, as a landscape accent stone.)

If you decide to incorporate big stones in a wall, chimney, or tower, be sure to position some of them up high, too. Many early builders used big rocks down low, but only small ones they could handle when they got up higher. You want yours spread out over the whole expanse.

The procedure is to select a big stone, then lay a supporting base of stones for it. If it has a curve or slope, build in the matching base. Then, after this work has cured for at least two days, you're ready to lay the big one on top. Dry-fit it carefully, using whatever means you have for lifting it. We frequently use webbed nylon slings rather than chains and the boom, so we can set the stone and then lift it easily to mortar the bed and make any corrections necessary.

You'll have to pry up the big stone to slide out the sling or chain if you've lifted it into position that way. There are devices for clamping the stones, but they usually leave scars. And if you lift by hand, all of you will have to get your fingers out of the way, or that will leave scars, too. I use a wooden block, which I take out with a crowbar when everything is set.

As an alternative, you can load the big rock into a tractor or loader bucket, raise it to height, then slide it into its place with crowbars. This is messier once the mortar is on, however. If you have neither bucket nor sling, you can work the stone up a beam and into place, but there are more chances that something will slip, break, or come loose. You also can rig a tripod over a wall that is out in the open and lift the stones with a come-along.

If you're veneering a wall, set scaffolding close and hang a hoist from a beam, so that you can swing the stone up and then guide it into place. Here again, a boom is handy because it can be maneuvered to pick up the stone, swing it in a wide arc if necessary, and place it in position, using the cable winch to lower it.

If you are manipulating the big one by hand with help, have room for everyone to get around it. Set it on the mortar bed and shim if necessary with stone chips to keep it plumb. You can knock these out after the mortar cures; if you've had to fill a wide

Filling Wide Mortar Joints with Chips or Shims

No matter how careful you are, there will be wide mortar surfaces in your work, especially if you use large stones. This usually happens where an even corner wasn't there in the rock you laid, or a tapered stone left a wedge-shaped expanse.

- Try to make chips look structural. For example, if there's a triangle of mortar, I use a matching stone triangle. A square chip in a triangular space is never good.
- Be sure any chip you use is deep enough to stay in place, usually at least two inches. Push the chip into the mortar within two hours of laying the stone. If the mortar is too hard to push the chip into it, rake it out, push more fresh mortar in, and wedge in the chip. Pack the mortar around it with a pointing tool.
- Avoid using more than two chips together. Sometimes you'll need a long, thin chip, and you probably won't find it in the scraps you have from your shaping of stones. I find or shape two chips and wedge them in so they look like one.
- It's a mistake to lay stone with so wide a mortar joint that you must rely on filling heavily with chips. Take more time to dry-fit the stones in the first place.
- Recess the mortar around the chips just as you would elsewhere. And be sure the face of each chip is flush with that of the wall.

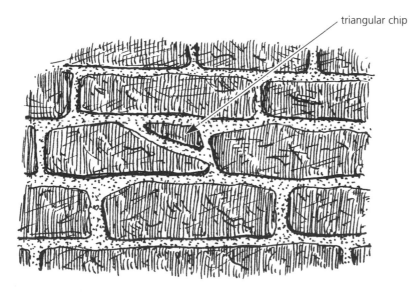

triangular chip

In filling wide mortar joints, shape the chip to match the shape of the joint.

In circular or sharply curved walls — as in this stair tower — long, straight stones must be laid vertically.

spot, just leave them in. Next to a big stone, chips just don't show up unless you've gone crazy with too many of them.

The next job is to adapt the rest of the wall to the big one. If it's tall, you'll necessarily have a vertical running joint up each edge of the large stone, which means you'll have to bridge the stone at the top. Match edges of the smaller flanking stones to the big one, and come out even horizontally for this bridging. Try to use substantial stones next to big ones so that they don't look like freaks. For example, a six-foot face might have some two- and three-foot stones next to it. Odd-shaped stones, too, must be matched closely to adjoining stone edges to keep them from looking like mistakes.

My wife liked a long stone we wanted to put into our stair tower. Since the stone didn't curve, it had to go in vertically, creating tall running joints, which traditionally are to be avoided. But once surrounded and bridged, it looks fine. In other places, we used long stones that were curved horizontally.

It's much simpler to use a long stone laid horizontally rather than vertically. It will look better, usually, since that's the way rocks are in nature, and it's easier to hold in place. In veneer work, you'll be using corrugated masonry ties, but they don't work until there's cured mortar between the stones. So you may have to prop up a tall stone while you work around it.

And that violates a basic tenet of stonework: No stone should be put anywhere that it won't stay by itself. So make sure tall stones are shaped to their beds and can stand in place before mortaring.

It's a good idea to break up a horizontal ledge pattern with a triangle or parallelogram or a curved edge, but if it doesn't fit,

Large and odd-shaped stones add interest to this granite retaining wall in central Virginia.

it's a mistake. Even if it's in a veneer wall, each stone must look as if it's holding up the structure.

There's another advantage to using large stones: The joints may have to be wider, but no one will notice. If you're working toward a half-inch joint, you can get by with a one-inch joint next to a huge stone, because the eye goes to the stone, not to the joint.

A trademark in our stonework is the use of big stones. The real reason is appearance, since that's the principal reason for using stone in the first place. And veneer or not, any stone properly laid looks as though it is heavy and deep, massive and strong. A big one appears even more so.

Accent Stones in Landscaping

In landscaping, monolithic stones should appear to be natural. For example, an irregularly shaped stone with moss on it is more appropriate than a stone whose shape is better suited to a wall. And the bigger the better, because the stone should appear to be an outcropping, or the base of the hill itself.

I recall a man I worked for in Harrison, Arkansas, many years ago. He had seen some of my stonework and asked what he could do to accent a long, freshly bulldozed driveway. I told him to use big stones and plantings and to make everything look like it had always been there.

You always lose something in translation. The next time I saw his driveway, he'd had someone haul in huge, round, clay-stained boulders dug up from somewhere. They were lined up, nose to nose, along the drive. That was over thirty years ago; I'll go back someday and see if they've aged.

I do occasionally age some select stones. A corner of our house sits where there was a pile of huge granite stones, old broken plowpoints, and briars. We dug them out, piled them down in the woods, and now, fourteen years later, they have moss and lichen on them. Just right for accent stones in a garden.

The giant stones of the Egyptian pyramids and of Chichén Itzá in Mexico were used because they were all there was to build with that would be permanent. For centuries, people have wondered how the builders shaped and moved such large stones. The answer is: lots of help, under whatever circumstances, and lots of time.

Stones are all about time — time to find them, to move them, to place them, and time, occasionally, to chisel and shape them (the subject of the next chapter).

And above all, time to see them, experience them, and fall under their spell.

This large landscaping stone stands in gravel, beside plantings and pool, in Greene County, Virginia.

Mason Eric Bolton builds a drystone retaining wall. Here he cuts an end off to improve the fit.

CHAPTER 5

Cutting and Shaping Stone

WE'RE TALKING ABOUT FIELDSTONE here, so forget about those identically faced blocks that you see on old storefronts, arched bridges, and door and window lintels. The intention then was to have a smooth facade that looked as little like stone as possible. In this book, however, we're celebrating stone as a natural material, so we'll do only a minimal amount of shaping.

In general, good fieldstone masons will only true up — that is, make level or plumb — the shapes they find, not try to create new ones. A long, triangle-faced stone might get its corners chipped to match others in a wall. Or a curved edge could get straightened for a better fit in a ledge pattern. A thick stone might need to be split for veneer work — and if you're lucky, you get two stones. Minimal shaping is always recommended because newly cut stone faces glare from an aged wall. It takes years for these fresh cuts to blend in, so try to avoid them where they will show.

Hammer and Chisel

To cut a corner off a stone, lay it on something soft to absorb the shock. Sand in a box is good, or use a table padded with old rugs. Try to get the work area elevated to about counter height (thirty-six inches), or you can follow the blacksmith's rule of thumb for his anvil: the height of your knuckles when standing with arms dangling. Bending down to work at ground level is hard.

Now, to mark the cut you want, make a series of light hits with a striking hammer on a stone chisel, then go over this line again, this time striking harder. After about the third pass, turn

Hammer and chisel can be used to shape stone. The pointed end of this stone has begun to crack off, leaving a square edge.

Splitting stone can often be done with a chisel along the grain. Mark first with light hammer blows, then repeat with more force until the stone splits.

the stone over and mark that side, too. Repeat the procedure, using more force with each repetition. If you're working near the edge of the stone, lean the chisel out a bit to direct it into the mass of the stone. (If you hold it perpendicular, the stone will tend to chip off instead of breaking all the way through.)

One thing to remember: A light tap will tend to chip the stone out toward the edge. A heavier hit will crack it deeper, usually closer to where you want it. Sometimes the stone will break toward the edge anyway, leaving a ridge on the edge face. Slope the chisel sharply, just enough for it to bite into the surface, striking into the mass near the ridge. Take small chips off from both sides this way until you have dressed the surfaces sufficiently. Ideally, the stone will break all the way through from marked line to line, but don't count on it the first few thousand times.

Occasionally you can shape a thin edge with just the mason's hammer because the sharp effect of striking from a swing is different from that of hitting a stationary chisel. A mason's hammer is usually less accurate than a chisel, but it's faster and lets you hold the stone in place with your other hand.

A large stone-breaking maul, which has an edge to it, will create small stones from big ones, and I sometimes use a twelve-pounder for this if there's no way to utilize big stones as they are. Hit a line lightly, as with the chisel, then go back over it harder. You'll have to smooth your breaks afterward with the hammer and chisel, because the maul gives you approximates only. Splitting sedimentary stones, such as sandstone and limestone, is quick with a maul if your aim is good. It's a lot like splitting wood, but it doesn't go quite as quickly. I knew a man who split the rounded sandstone from the river at his farm in the Shenandoah Valley. The new faces showed nice colors, but they were difficult to lay, being rounded on the backs.

I don't use diamond-tooth saws to shape stones because I don't want edges that are too straight or too sharp. It's a matter of style. We did a job once with a mason who cut the edges of his arch fieldstones with a saw. It took as long as it did for Dan Smith, who was working with me, to shape his with the chisel. The chiseled cuts looked better.

The Elusive "Perfect Fit"

Masons have always been fascinated by cutting mortises and steps in stones for the perfect fit. It's rarely worth the time it takes, and too often a stone breaks after hours of shaping. Try to use the spaces between stones creatively rather than go for a tight fit every time. Often, you can proceed much more efficiently on a job if you lay a stone that leaves a space you can fill with a shim or chip. But I don't recommend that you do this too often.

Chisel Safety Tips

Watch the condition of stone chisels, particularly the struck ends. These will mushroom from repeated striking with the hammer. And if a flying stone chip is painful, I can tell you a bit of steel shrapnel from a chisel is many times worse. It will tear its way right through cloth to find your flesh. I don't want to think what it could do to an unprotected eye, so be sure you always wear goggles when using or grinding stone chisels.

Grind the ragged edges off your chisels as you notice them forming. And if the chisel head does *not* mushroom in use, be wary: It may be too hard to spread and therefore hard enough to shatter.

And, of course, just as every carpenter misses the nail eventually, you will miss the chisel and slam your hand. I have a network of scars on my holding hand. Gloves help a bit, but they won't prevent smashed fingers.

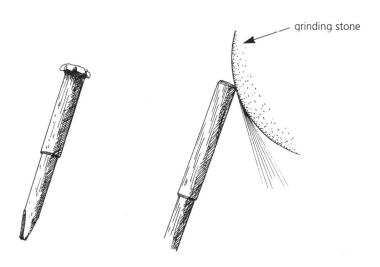

grinding stone

The struck end of the chisel on the left has begun to mushroom, while the ragged edge of the chisel on the right also requires grinding.

The dry-stack look, which is popular right now, requires closer fitting and therefore more shaping. Dry-stack is mortared stone, but none of the mortared joints shows, so it looks like tightly laid drystone work. Sometimes it will allow more chips and shims, sometimes not. If large stones are required for a job, there are just two solutions: Search more or shape more.

For a tight fit at the edges, you may have to take down a hump. To do this, stand the stone on edge and dress the offending surface with a chisel or a stone point, which is just what it sounds like: a chisel that comes to a point. It is used to chip off bits of stone. Slow, but it works.

The most important thing to remember about shaping stones: Don't attempt it unless you must. If you have a lot of extra stone, you may be able to find the right fit, even if you must use two or more to fill the gap. You'll find cutting frustrating enough to want to avoid it, even with easily shaped sandstone. If you're using granites, just find the right ones.

Complex cutting and shaping by master stonemasons united intersecting mortared arches into a vaulted ceiling in the ruins of St. Leonard's Hospital in York, England.

Demand your own best work. You'll find some frustration in fitting stones and that will inevitably result in your using some that you shouldn't. Fight the tendency to lay a stone that's just "good enough." It won't look any better as time passes. Sloppy work will haunt you. As you become more proficient, your early work will look bad enough to you even if it's acceptable. If it's really bad, it'll be a constant embarrassment.

So take time to find the right stone, or shape it when absolutely necessary. Keep joints tight, faces plumb. Stand back often and use a critical eye on your work. If something needs fixing, do it now. It's much easier to take out a mortared-in stone and replace it now if it's wrong. Later, it's much, much more difficult.

Of the dozens of masons I know, most do some minimal shaping of about half the stones they lay. Some never cut a stone; some compulsively shape every stone they lay. I find myself searching, saving time by doing some shaping on perhaps a third of the stones I put in place. Time is the key word here, as it is in every aspect of stonework: You decide how tight you want a joint and whether you'll shape a stone or look for a better fit. Or just leave it a bit loose.

This dry-stack restoration basement wall, mortared with no mortar showing, was rebuilt to look exactly like the original. Each stone was numbered and coded from the original structure.

Commercial Cutting, Past and Present

Commercial quarrying was done traditionally by drilling lines of holes in the stone with star drills (four-ribbed punches sharpened at the end) and hammers. Feathers — half-round metal pieces — were then placed in the holes and wedges were driven between them. Applying roughly equal pressure to all the wedges eventually cracked the stone in a straight line. A variation of this technique involves driving wooden plugs into these holes, then dripping water on them. Strange as it may sound, the expanding cells in the wood can crack off big stones.

Pneumatic and electric drills have replaced the star drill, but stone is still shaped this way. For big jobs, the holes are filled with explosives and the stone is blown apart. This "shot" stone often has hairline cracks in it and is not the best for masonry. But it's still used, and with age it can look good.

Too often, masons choose the latter course, and that is what separates them from master masons. Remember how long mistakes will be there, visible. Better to take a bit more time now, while you can. You're building for posterity, after all.

With minimal cutting and shaping, these became wonderful building stones, just large enough to be impressive and fill large amounts of space, but small enough not to daunt the stonebuilder.

PART 2

Stonework Projects

Everyone who drives by is impressed by this wall's 160-foot length and beautiful workmanship. This modern, mortared freestanding wall, built by Ned Horn, borders a Virginia estate.

CHAPTER 6

Basic and Inspired Walls

EVERY STONE STRUCTURE I can think of starts with a wall. A stone pier is a short wall. A gateway, an arched foundation, a chimney — all are walls. Flying buttresses are walls to begin with.

The first thing you need to learn when working with stone, then, is how to build a basic wall. In general, it is simply the act of placing stones on top of other stones, with some intelligent constraints. (If it falls down, for instance, it isn't a wall.)

Drystone Freestanding Walls

I teach my apprentice masons to first lay drystone walls. The principle is that a stone should stay in place without mortar, because gravity and friction will hold it in place when it is laid properly.

So, if it's a freestanding wall, it should have stones on each face that slope inward against each other to ensure that wayward tourists and other large animals won't push it over. Each stone, if possible, should push against its neighbor in a controlled situation that doesn't let either move. Now, if you were to follow this religiously, in cross section you'd have two walls, leaning into each other. This doesn't work too well, however, because either of the two can come apart in other ways. To compensate, we tie clear across the wall whenever we can with a tie-stone, giving a platform for the next pair up.

Tie-stones are laid completely flat, or they'll creep downhill with freezes and thaws. They're especially important for capping the wall, for they hold it together and keep out rain, which will freeze and push the wall apart. Capstones also make it more difficult for dust, leaves, and other debris to blow into the wall, where they can nurture tree seeds. Allowing tree roots to sprout in your wall is guaranteed to force it apart.

For tie-stones to work, the wall thickness has to be manageable, and there are lots of formulas: The thickness can be half the height, one-third the height, equal to the height. This ratio depends on how "good" the stones are. In this instance, we'll use the mason's definition of a good stone: one that is level on top and bottom so that it will lie flat and support maximum weight. With good tops and bottoms, stones can stay put with a thickness that is easily half the wall height. So a four-foot wall, for example, can be two feet thick, and it's not impossible to find two-foot-wide rocks to tie across with.

How do we get most of these stones to slope inward? We start by digging the topsoil away at the base of the wall in a shallow V-shape. Then we lay flat, roughly twelve-inch-wide stones (for our hypothetical two-foot-thick wall) from the center to the outside edge of the V. A slope of one inch down to the point of the V is enough to encourage the stones to move toward each other. You see, when you use a tie-stone, it probably won't have a convenient dip in the middle, so the shallower the V-slope, the better the tie-stones fit. Try to use tie-stones for every third course.

More than likely, your supply of neat stones two feet wide (or long) with nice edges will be limited or nonexistent, so you'll have to shape at least one end for a face. That means you'll need longer stones to start with.

It's simpler to build a drystone wall with thin stones, because they're easier to handle and can be shaped better than thick ones. But if you have only thick stones, take the time to shape good end faces. If you want a really rustic look, don't worry about the tie-stone ends. If you've been careful to align the outer edges of the other stones in the wall (the ideal twelve-inch ones), the tie-stone ends can vary in appearance

This drystone wall in Pennsylvania took the farmer years to build as he cleared his fields.

and overhang without looking too sloppy. After all, the surface of a stone wall is never even. If you have established a plane that you go back to often, you can take some liberties with it.

Those twelve-inch sloped stones that touch in the center of the wall won't be ideal, either. Lay them with the best edges out, and if that leaves gaps in the center of the wall, fill these with rubble — that is, any scrap stone not usable otherwise. Stone chips and small rubble pieces are also good to level up the V-slope for a tie-stone.

After you've tied the wall with a tie-stone — which you try to do about every four feet along the wall — you'll have to reestablish the V-slope with the next course. Tapered stones are the obvious answer, or you can wedge up the outside edges with chips. Chips, or shims, must not be tapered, however, or they will work out with the flexing of drystone work. Use thin rectangular chips from your shapings or break thin stones for shims. Properly laid, wedged stones won't shift, even when used as steps, where they get jostled a lot.

Always lay stones side by side with the top edge parallel to the ground, and make sure to cover the crack between them with a stone on the next course. If you don't, you'll have a running joint, or vertical crack, which will weaken the wall too much. A joint that is two courses deep is permissible but not desirable.

When building a drystone wall that runs downhill, keep the stones level. This requires removing the topsoil at the base of the

Regardless of the type of wall you're building, avoid vertical running joints. In this wall, notice how each course overlaps the cracks in the preceding layer.

The eye initially focuses on the dominant plane of a wall rather than on any surface unevenness. Stones may jut out or be recessed, as long as a plane is established and vertical running joints avoided, as in this drystone wall built by students.

Whether a freestanding wall is drystone or mortared, many of the same basic principles apply. As this mortared wall in Highland County, Virginia, illustrates, hill walls must be stepped, and capstones should cover as much surface area as possible.

wall in a stepped pattern and repeating this pattern with the capstones. Stones that slope or are laid at an angle will move over time, and even though it may take them a while to do this, you don't want your wall to fall down. Build it right the first time so that future generations will have to repair only damage done accidentally by swinging brush-hogs or backing minivans.

Capstones are the crowning touch for a stone wall, and consequently it is good practice to obtain a supply of them before you even start building the wall. Keep in mind that you *don't* want protruding ends or gaps you can't quite cover. And you must cover as many cracks in the wall as possible so that rainwater won't get in, freeze, and push the wall apart.

As you collect prime capstone candidates, resist the urge to use them occasionally as tie-stones. The capstone is, of course, the top tie-stone, and it should be as large as possible. This means it covers more area, and its weight alone keeps it in place in drystone construction.

A well-laid drystone wall is attractive to behold. Lichens and even mosses will grow on the stones if there's enough moisture in the soil. (If it's a retaining wall, moisture will seep out of the soil it's holding in place.) Eventually, even the fresh breaks and cuts you've had to make at the ends of the tie-stones will age and blend. Achieving this permanently beautiful structure is something in which you can take undiminished pride.

Drystone Freestanding Wall

A freestanding wall, 3 ft. (0.9m) high and 2 ft. (0.6m) thick

MATERIALS

- 1 ton (0.9 t) of relatively flat (tops and bottoms) stones, 6–24 in. (15–62 cm) wide and 2–6 in. (5–15 cm) thick, for every 3 ft. (0.9 m) of wall length

TOOLS

pick
shovel
wheelbarrow
stone chisel
striking hammer
mason's hammer

pry bar (straight or crowbar)
four-foot level
tape

A freestanding drystone wall is the simplest and most attractive structure you can build of stone. There's no footing, no mortar, no cracking with freezing. If you use stones gathered from the top of the ground, they'll have lichens and an aged appearance. So a new drystone wall will look as if it's centuries old.

1. Dig a shallow trench 24 in. (0.6 m) wide to subsoil (4–6 in. [10–15 cm]) with a slight V-slope, deeper by about 2 in. (5 cm) in the center. Keep the ditch level lengthwise; if the ground slopes, step the trench to stay level.

2. Place stones along the bottom of the trench in pairs, with each sloping toward the center. Use stones that have a relatively even outside edge and that reach near the center of the trench. If a stone extends 2–3 in. (5–8 cm) past the center, adjust the soil for it, and use a narrower one opposite it. If both stones are short, fill the center space with broken stones.

Place uneven surfaces down on this first course, digging out as necessary. Leave as smooth a top surface as possible, matching stone heights.

3. Begin the next course with similar stones, taking care to cover the cracks between the first-layer stones. If you have spanned the 24 in. (0.6 m) trench with one 15 in. (0.4 m) stone on, say, the right side and a 9 in. (0.2 m) one on the left, reverse this now. If the stones were 12 in. (0.3 m) long (along the length of the wall), use shorter or larger ones on this second layer to avoid vertical running joints. Try to use stones of uniform thickness (height) in each course. Where this is impossible, use two thin ones alongside a thick one for an even height.

4. Wedge wherever necessary for solidity, using nontapered shims to prevent their working out as the wall flexes.

wedge

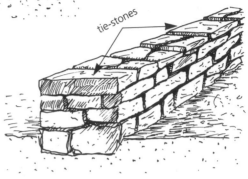

tie-stones

5. Use the four-foot level to keep the wall vertical. Place a 24 in. (0.6 m) stone every third or fourth layer as a tie-stone. Since this will be seen on both wall faces, it should have relatively straight ends. Use the hammer and chisel if necessary to shape these faces. There should be a tie-stone about every 4 ft. (1.2 m) along the length of the wall. Reestablish your V-slope after each course, as necessary.

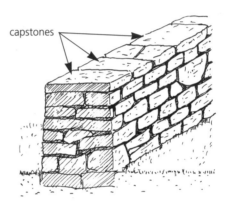

capstones

6. Use as many tie-stones as possible for the top layer. These are called capstones, and they are easily dislodged unless large and heavy. The best stones should be saved for capstones, since piecing this top layer will make it unstable.

7. Remember, if the wall goes up- or downhill, you must step the top, as you did the trench at the beginning, to keep it level.

8. Begin and end the wall vertically (A), or step it down to the ground (B). If the ground rises, keep the wall top level until it fades into the grade (C).

A

B

C

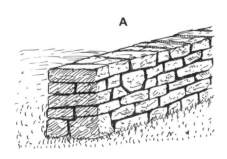

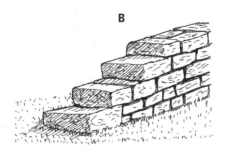

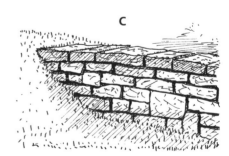

Mortared Walls

A mortared wall seals out water and roots, does not flex appreciably with temperature changes, and is much stronger than a drystone wall. It's more than a dry wall with cement in it, however. Since it cannot flex, mortared stonework must be set on a footing (preferably concrete) that extends below the frost line. The footing can be as high as the surface of the ground, or six inches below it. A footing distributes the weight of the wall over a wider area, reducing the downward pressure of this weight. It is more important for it to be wide rather than deep. Building codes vary, but usually anything that requires a foundation requires a building permit.

A four-foot mortared stone wall can be narrower than a comparable drystone wall. A width of 18 inches provides adequate stability for a straight wall; if the wall curves or has supporting buttresses or angles in it, it can be as narrow as 12 inches. The footing should be twice the width of the wall thickness.

Concrete Footings

Dig a ditch to below frost line in your area. Step the ditch if the wall will go down a slope. Step heights can vary, but because concrete blocks are commonly used, most are eight inches. Put steps in place using boards set in grooves in the sides of the ditch and braced with short pieces of reinforcing rod.

Rebar grade stakes will be required by the building inspector to determine the footing thickness. These are driven down

---

Mixing Concrete

The basic mix is:

- 1 part Portland cement
- 2 parts sand
- 3 parts gravel, 1 in. (2.5 cm) or less in size (what quarries call six-to-eights)

Mix concrete footings in small quantities in a wheelbarrow or in a portable mixer. Start with the sand, then add the Portland cement, which typically comes in cubic-foot sacks weighing 94 lbs. (42.6 kg). Dry mix, then add water until the mix is wet and loose. How much water you need varies a lot, a key factor being how dry or wet the sand is when you start. Add the gravel last, working it into the wet mix a little at a time.

Concrete should be dry enough to hold shaped peaks when you shovel it into place, but wet enough to level out when it is shaken with a hoe. If water puddles up on it, it is too wet. Excess water will leave air pockets when the concrete dries, which will weaken it.

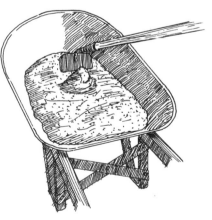

Concrete mixture should be firm enough to hold peaks.

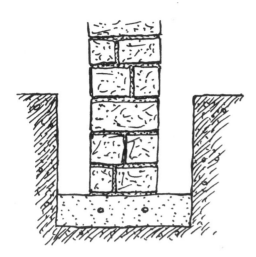

concrete footing reinforced with rebar

crushed-stone footing

every four feet or so, and their top ends leveled. You can use a four-foot level for this, or a line level, water level (hose full of water), or transit. The inspector will want to see these set, along with step bulkheads and smooth, solid ditch bottoms and sharp ditch corners, before he'll approve the pour.

The depth or thickness of the footing concrete is largely up to you, beyond the eight-inch minimum I'm recommending for our hypothetical four-foot-high wall. It is commonplace to lay concrete block below ground level instead of wasting good stones where they will not be seen. Really misshapen stones hidden down there won't hold up the wall properly, unless they're embedded in concrete. In our situation, it's actually cheaper to buy ready-mixed concrete and fill the ditch to ground level. Additional labor and materials to bring the wall up to the surface are too expensive.

If you're in a place a concrete truck can't get to and you're mixing footing concrete by hand or in a mixer, the equation can change, especially if your wall is going to be a long one, in which case it may take too much concrete to fill the ditch that way. If you have lots of good stone, you can afford to hide it belowground.

Let's do a purist scenario: You have enough rock to use the less-than-gorgeous ones belowground, the weather is dry, and it's above freezing. You're mixing your own footing concrete by hand or in a small mixer.

Calculate how much footing you'll need before you start. At three feet wide and eight inches deep, you'll be mixing and pouring two cubic feet per running foot of ditch. For a fifty-foot wall, that's a minimum of one hundred cubic feet of concrete (more, if it has steps in it). You'll do well to mix one cubic foot at a time by hand in a wheelbarrow, and two to three at a time in a small- to medium-size mixer. Start early, and be sure to have help. Also have on hand enough gravel, sand, and cement. For our hypothetical fifty-foot wall, you'd need about four cubic yards of gravel, allowing for spills and settling. That amounts to several loads in your pickup truck, so you might want to have the quarry deliver it. Its crushed rock generally makes stronger concrete than rounded creek gravel, too, although you can dig the latter yourself. Add to that two-thirds as much sand and about twenty-five cubic-foot sacks of Portland. You won't be able to use all the cement at once, so be sure to store it off the ground, wrapped in plastic or under a roof. Don't secure the plastic to the ground or ground moisture will condense under it and get the cement wet. And don't store Portland for more than a month. There's often enough moisture in the air to start the chemical process of setting up, which you don't want until after you mix and pour.

It's questionable whether you actually save significantly by mixing your own concrete. Ready-mix companies structure their prices just enough higher than the builder can do it in order to get the business, throwing in speed and convenience as additional incentives. At present I pay sixty-five dollars a cubic yard (0.8 cu m) for concrete. If I have a big pour (my biggest was 44 yards), there's no way I can mix it myself cheaply or on time. But if I need a half-yard or less, that's another matter. Often when we build porches or stone piers, we'll dig the footings by hand and use maybe two wheelbarrow mixes for each footing.

Concrete pumping is convenient for sites that a truck can't get close to, but it's expensive. Count on a base charge of around four hundred dollars, plus mileage and a per-yard fee. Also, not every small-town operation has a pump truck.

McRaven Restorations crewman John Allietta protects himself from breathing cement and lime dust when he mixes concrete or mortar.

You'll need reinforcing rods, or rebar, typically half an inch thick, in the footing to strengthen it. Steel makes cement strong. Otherwise, soft spots in the ditch bottom, or places where it goes from bedrock to dirt, can settle and crack your stone wall. Set the rebar in the concrete halfway up the footing thickness. Don't prop the rod up on bricks or rocks, because that leaves a hairline crack for water to seep into, which will rust the steel. Pour four inches of concrete, then place two rods a foot apart in the center of your three-foot ditch. Overlap the rebar ends six inches. Then pour the rest of the footing.

Always try to pour the concrete all at once. If a section has as much as an hour to set up before you join it with another, you get a "cold" joint, which is another place for water to seep in and thus weaken the concrete. Establishing a rough level is close enough if you're laying stone on top of the footing, but it must be smoother for concrete block. I dump wheelbarrow loads in, then smooth them with a hoe. As you even out the surface, feel around for the tops of the rebar grade stakes.

Gravel Footings

Another type of footing that is much cheaper, but not as long lived or as strong, is a gravel footing. With this, you dig a ditch well below frost line but only as wide as your wall thickness. Then you dump in gravel or crushed stone to a minimum of six inches deep, but you must keep the top below frost line. Then you level off and start laying stone.

The theory here is that water won't get into the wall and freeze because the mortar seals it out. It doesn't freeze below the wall and buckle it because that's below frost line. And since the water soaks through the gravel and away quickly, the wall stays stable.

I've built mortared walls on this kind of footing, but there are two drawbacks: The footing does nothing to distribute the weight of the wall, so it can settle and, of course, crack. And eventually the gravel gets dirt washed into it, the water stops percolating through it, and the wall essentially sits on dirt. In addition, tree roots do a lot more damage when they can get under a wall this easily. But such a footing can serve you well for a long time. Given the expense of the concrete footing, the gravel-based wall may be the way to go. Cracks in the stonework don't mean that it's about to explode or anything like that. And if you're middle-aged when you build it, the wall will probably still look good when you're history.

Building with Mortar

I've included a lot about footings because this base is necessary for the really fine mortared wall. Early builders dug deep, then laid wide, flat stones down there, mortared to keep moisture out. Lots of their walls are still sound. But you'll probably have access to more concrete than good stone, so I recommend the concrete footing.

Whether you've built to ground level with concrete, concrete block, or stone, you're ready now to lay stone that will show. Your work will be judged by this, so it needs to be right. You have several styles to choose from but the stone itself will influence your decision. Rounded edges, for instance, preclude a tight, mortarless look. For strength, a basically horizontal or ledge pattern is best. Too many same-sized stones can look monotonous, so vary the sizes often. Just remember to return as much as is practical to the horizontal arrangement.

The idea here is to follow the principles of drystone work, minimizing mortar but sealing out water and making the wall rigid. You still want to cover vertical cracks to lock everything together. You also want to step hill walls and lay stones flat instead of up on edge unless they are very thick. Tie-stones are also essential.

Now, if this is a freestanding wall like our drystone one, it's easier to face both sides. We've already learned that the perfect tie-stone is a rare find, and mortar only helps that a little. With mortar we may extend a tie-stone a couple of inches across the joint left by two shallow stones below, and then use smaller pieces to fill the space out to the opposite side. Next course up, reverse this and come the other way. (You can do this with drystone, too, but it won't stay as well.)

If you've elected to try the dry-stack, mortarless look, you have a big job ahead of you. I don't teach this to beginners because it's a frustrating procedure. Better to aim for joints between half an inch and an inch, recessed deeply (one inch or so) so that they're not noticeable. A substantial mortar joint will bond well, keep out water better, and take up the irregularities in the stones more easily.

Many masons charge different square-foot prices for wide (one-inch), narrow, or mortarless joints. Generally, I will put a beginner on a job requiring one-inch joints, and a mason who's worked with me a year or more on half-inch joints. Only the top people and I do tight dry-stack. This isn't just because it's difficult to do, but also because it's extremely difficult to do *right*. I'll have more to say about this style later.

Spread one inch of mortar on the footing, holding it back about one inch from the face, and lay your first stone. Rock it just a bit to work out air pockets. If mortar gets pushed out to the face, trim it off and rake the joint out with the pointing tool. Don't let mortar get onto the stone faces at all; the stains are hard to get off.

The mortared wall at the rear of this yard and garden helps limit creek erosion, while the lower curved wall of similar stone is more ornamental than functional.

As with this wall at Bear Mountain, Virginia, alternate short and long stones to lock together freestanding vertical ends.

If your wall has a freestanding vertical end — if it doesn't end against a building or fade into the ground — alternate short and long stones so that the end is even but each course is locked together. It's like using half-bricks to end every other course. Bricklaying, by the way, evolved from stonework, and the principle is the same: Cover the crack between two stones with the stone above.

Lay several feet horizontally, working with the full width of the wall so that you create the outside faces together. Then go back and work on the second course. I like to do about three courses a day. You can lay the first one all the way to the end of the wall before you start the second, but you won't have much of a sense of progress in the beginning.

Most masons use stretched strings to keep the wall straight. Strings get in the way a lot, but using them is probably a good practice, especially for beginners. I don't use strings, but then I also lay up a two-story chimney without a level. I like stonework to be a bit less disciplined than brick, so I don't try to keep my walls gun-barrel straight and smooth.

Do use a level to stay vertical, however, because the ins and outs of irregular stone faces will fool you at first. Here, it's impossible to stay exactly even; you must judge how much you'll let a knob protrude past the wall plane, or how much of a recess will still give you a visually even wall surface. It's a matter of personal choice, unless you're doing the job for someone else. (By the way, don't do your first wall for someone else. Take a hint from the man who wanted to become an auto-body repairman: He practiced on the relics at the junkyard.)

It's a good idea to dry-fit a few stones to see how they look before you actually mortar them. Don't do too many, though, for the mortar will change the dimensions. Then set this half dozen or so, rake the excess mortar from the joints, and stand back and admire your handiwork. The secret to avoiding intimidation by all the stone that has to be laid is to concentrate on what you have accomplished, not on what you have left to do. Rome was built one rock at a time, believe me.

When you stop for the day, leave stone in steps, rather than leaving a vertical end, so it's easier to tie onto next time. Fill any wide mortar joints with appropriately shaped chips. There will be a lot of bits from your shaping, but few of them will be shaped like the places they will fill. Triangles are most in demand, because not every stone you've laid will have a nice, squared-off end. So lay an almost-good stone, and count on a shim to take up the slack.

Rake the joints to a uniform depth of about one inch at the end of the day. The morning's work will be crumbly, but the later work may try to smear; so wait until the next morning to

Mixing Mortar for Stonework

A heavy contractor's wheelbarrow is ideal for mixing mortar. You can move it to the sandpile, to where your Portland cement and lime are stored, and to the part of the site you're working on. The basic mix for stonework is:

- 1 part lime
- 2 parts Portland cement
- 9 parts sand

Cement typically comes in sacks weighing 94 lb. (42.6 kg); lime, in sacks of 50 lb. (22.7 kg). Start with the sand and add the Portland cement and lime, so that the wheelbarrow is no more than half full. A medium-size shovel used for the measuring produces a good batch of mortar.

Mix dry first, using the shovel, a hoe, or both. Then move the dry mix away from one end of the wheelbarrow pan and pour in about half a gallon (1.9 l) of water.

With the hoe, begin "chopping off" thin slices of the dry mix into the water. Work each bit until it's wet throughout, then chop some more. When this water is used up, open a hole beyond the mixed mortar for more water, and repeat the process. Be sure you don't leave dry pockets of mix down in the corners as you go. When you get to the end of the wheelbarrow with this process, you should be finished. Take care not to add too much water at a time or the mix can get overly wet. It should stand in peaks.

If the sand is wet from rain, you'll need very little water for the mix. As you get near the end of the batch, use only a small amount of water at a time. It's easy to go from too dry to too wet with just a cupful of water.

The consistency should be as wet as possible without running or dripping. Most masons use very dry mortar because it is neat and easy to clean up later, but it does not bond well to the stone. And water leaks through this dry mortar, which is embarrassing inside a stone house.

If the mix is too wet, add sand, Portland cement, and lime in proportionate amounts and mix until the batch stiffens up. Or you can leave it for 20 minutes or so, until water floats to the surface. Pour this off and repeat. The mortar at the bottom will thicken enough for use, and you can scrape the soft stuff aside to get to it.

As you use the mortar, it will dry out more. This will get rid of too-wet mortar and will mean you have to add water to an ideal mix. Use all mortar within 2 hours of mixing.

The typical work site is a long term commitment of space, and is not always tidy. It takes much more stone than you think to do any job because you'll want to have choices for your work. You'll need space for the stone, the sand supply, and a mixing box or wheelbarrow, as well as space to move.

Mix mortar by "chopping off" slices of the dry mixture and working each slice with water.

get those places. Then use a wire brush to clean up and make the mortar neat. Wet it thoroughly afterward, using any method you like, when you're sure that the mortar is dry enough not to run down the faces of the stones.

Moisture is important to curing mortar, which is a chemical process that goes on for several days. If the mortar dries out too soon, the process stops and the stuff has little strength. So wet it thoroughly about four times during the day after you lay mortared stone. In very hot weather, drape plastic sheeting over it to hold the moisture in. After two days it doesn't matter much; the process naturally slows down.

With mortared work, wall capstones need not be full width, but it's better if they are. Mortar erodes, so the bigger the capstones, the better: less mortar to weather away. Don't recess the joints on top; you'll need all the holding power of the mortar at the edges of the stones.

Raking Mortar Joints

No matter how deeply you want the mortar joints struck, this depth should be consistent. It's probably impossible to use just the right quantity of mortar every time, so count on raking some out.

I do this shortly after I lay each stone, using the pointing tool to rake it out onto a trowel for reuse. It's usually wet enough to smear if you try to do a complete cleanup now, however.

Six to 12 hours after laying, the joints can still be raked, and at this time a wire-brush cleanup is in order. Raking will leave grooves, pits, and uneven places, but the wire brush will smooth them.

After the mortar has had a few hours to set up, a good mason will clean the joints of any excess mortar. Here, a mason uses a pointing tool to rake out the joints.

Just as your wall began with a vertical end, it can end the same way, or it can taper out into rising ground. Don't stop it against a tree, or the roots will break it apart. You can terminate a wall at a square pillar, as in a gateway, or switch to a fence at the end.

Cleaning Mortar from Stones

First, don't let mortar get onto stone faces, if at all possible. Mix dry, and keep mortar dry enough that it won't run. That's a bit tricky, because it has to be wet enough to bond to the stone surfaces. Stone laid up with very dry mortar comes apart. The mortar should be stiff enough that peaks don't shake down flat unless vibrated very hard.

On a misty day, though, or after you may have cooled stone hot from the sun with water, you may get a run you didn't expect. Use a sponge while the mortar is still wet. If a stain or film of mortar shows up after the work has dried, the job is more difficult.

Enough scrubbing with water and a wire brush will eventually remove dried stains, but there's an easier way. Use 1 part muriatic acid to 10 parts of water to remove stains. It won't work on built-up mortar — you'll have to scrape or chisel this off first. Repeat the acid treatment until the stain is gone. Flush with lots of water after about 30 minutes. You can find muriatic acid at the masonry supply store.

If you're trying to keep lichens or moss alive on the stones, don't use the acid. Even the mortar will kill these plants, so be very careful when you handle these stones.

A wire brush and water will eventually remove dried mortar stains from stone.

Mortared Stone Freestanding Wall

A freestanding mortared wall, 3 ft. (0.9 m) high and 1 ft. (0.3 m) thick

MATERIALS

- 1 ton (0.9 t) of stone up to 12 in. (0.3 m) wide, varying thickness and length, with as many square, flat surfaces as possible, for every 6 *ft.* (1.8 m) of wall
- Concrete: about 2½ cu. ft. (71 cu dm) ready-mixed concrete for every 1 ft. (0.3 m) of wall length, or about 1 cu. yd. (0.8 cu m) for every 10 ft. (3 m) of wall. If you choose to mix the concrete yourself, you'll need about 1 cu. yd. (0.8 cu m) gravel, ⅔ cu. yd. (0.5 cu m) sand, and 9 sacks Portland cement for every 10 ft. (3 m) of wall.

- Mortar: 3 sacks Portland cement, 1 sack mason's lime, and 1 ton (0.9 t) sand for every 12–15 ft. (3.7–4.6 m) of wall length, water
- If wall runs up- or downhill, 8 x 30 x 1 in. (21 x 76 x 2.5 cm) boards for bulkheads
- ½ in. (13 mm) reinforcing rod, sold in 20 ft. (6 m) lengths; to be set in pairs into the footing running the full length of the wall
- Rebar grade stakes, 1 for each 4 ft. (1.2 m) of wall length

TOOLS

two 48 in. (1.2 m) stakes (one at each end for layout string to maintain a straight wall)
string
wheelbarrow
pick
shovel
hoe
large trowel
⅜ in. (1 cm) pointing tool
wire brushes
stone chisel
striking hammer
mason's hammer
pry bar
four-foot level
tape

A freestanding wall of mortared stone has the advantage of strength. Being sealed at the joints, it keeps water out, which could freeze and push stone apart. Properly laid on a footing and with joints raked ½–1 in. (13–25 mm) deep to let the stones stand out, a mortared wall is very atractive.

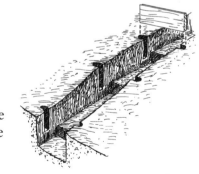

1. Dig a trench to below frost level 24 in. (0.6 m) wide. If the wall runs up- or downhill, step it to keep it level. Steps may be of any height, but 8 in. (21 cm) is customary. Set bulkhead boards into grooves cut into sides of the trench. If necessary, brace with wooden stakes driven into side trench walls. Drive in rebar grade stakes, one every 4 ft. (1.2 m) along the trench to the height you will fill with concrete.

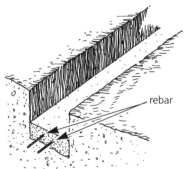

rebar

2. Pour concrete at least 6 in. (15 cm) deep in the trench for the footing. Fill the trench to the surface of the ground, if desired. The quantities given here assume you will dig to 18 in. (0.5 m) and fill to grade. You can substitute 12 in. (0.3 m) concrete blocks or stone below grade, on the footing. It is quicker and not too much more expensive to fill the trench to grade.

If you mix the footing concrete yourself, start with 2 shovels of cement, 4 of sand, and 6 of gravel, plus water (see "Mixing Concrete" page 65). In soft ground or where the trench goes from solid rock to soil, lay two ½ in. (13 mm) reinforcing rods (rebar) side by side, 8 in. (0.2 m) apart, midway in the depth of the concrete. Pour concrete level. It should reach the tops of the stepped bulkhead boards, if any.

3. After 2 days, remove bulkhead boards. Dry-fit 3–4 ft. (0.9–1.2 m) of wall length, keeping outside faces even and top surfaces level. Be sure each stone will stay in place dry. Shape with hammer and chisel where necessary. Leave ½ in. (13 mm) space between each stone. You may use two stones for the 12 in. (0.3 m) wall thickness.

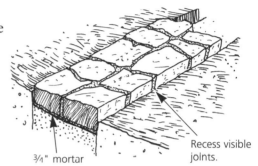

4. Mix mortar (see "Mixing Mortar for Stonework," page 71), then lay a base of ¾ in. (2 cm) of mortar on the concrete footing, removing and replacing the prefitted stones as you go. Fill between the stones, using the pointing tool to push mortar off the trowel into the crack. Recess visible joints at least ½ in. (13 mm). You may extend the first course as far as you like before beginning the second one. Keep the mortar wet for at least 2 days.

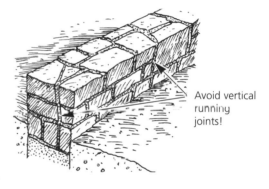

¾" mortar

Recess visible joints.

5. For the second and succeeding courses, avoid exterior and interior vertical running joints, just as in drystone work. Here, too, tie-stones are necessary. For this narrow wall, there will probably be no need to fill the center with small pieces. Fill small gaps with mortar, for strength. Work out all air spaces by packing with the pointing tool.

Avoid vertical running joints!

6. Within 4 hours of applying mortar, with the pointing tool rake out the joints to a uniform depth. Use the wire brush for additional cleaning up after the mortar is dry enough not to smear. Keep wet with a spray, or slosh water on, for at least 2 days. Normally 4 or 5 wettings a day will suffice.

7. Check vertical faces with the level. You may also stretch guide strings to keep your wall straight. Use tall stakes driven into the ground, and elevate the strings as necessary.

8. A mortared hill wall need not be stepped on top. The individual courses should be level, and if odd-shaped accent stones are used, return to a level again. If the top is to be sloped instead of stepped, you must use sloped stones — those thicker on one edge. The mortar will hold these in place, where dry capstones would dislodge.

It isn't necessary for all the capstones to be large and heavy, since they are mortared in place, but make sure mortared joints are tight, so that water won't get into the wall and freeze. If it does, stones will break off the wall.

Once you've mastered the basic wall, you can do a variety of things with it — you can bend it, angle it, put piers in it, curve it into a serpentine shape. Some of this is structural: When you change direction with a wall, it braces it. You can also do this with buttresses or curves. Piers, which in this case are thicker sections of the wall, do this to some degree, but being only slightly wider than the basic wall, they're more ornamental than strengthening.

Curved Walls

There are some treatments that just seem to belong to stone walls. One is curves: A curved stone wall brings to mind medieval castle towers and meandering pasture walls. A curved wall encloses space and gives a sense of shelter. Often a wall built between two existing features, such as a stone outcropping and a building, has added beauty if it curves. Lay out the curved perimeter with a piece of string staked to a center point. Give it a proportion that relates to the surroundings. The curved wall should also have a reason for curving: to contain, to exclude, to go around something natural.

More than eight feet tall, this curved retaining wall will eventually support a restored building.

This curved wall by Mike Firkaly functions as both a retaining wall and a freestanding wall to create a level area near a riverbank.

Curved Freestanding Wall

A curved wall or wall segment, drystone or mortared

MATERIALS
- Same as for basic drystone or mortared wall (see pages 62 or 74, respectively)

TOOLS
Same as for basic drystone or mortared wall with the addition of string and stakes to scribe the curve(s) and a small quantity of mason's lime

A curved stone wall is more self-supporting than a straight one, because no matter which way side force is applied, part of the wall must lift for it to move. The curve acts much like a corner or buttress to strengthen the wall. The ultimate curved wall is a serpentine wall, which is very strong, but often appears as an architectural oddity.

1. Lay out each curve for the wall using a stake as a pivoting point for a string. Experiment with locating the stake and string until you get just the right starting and finish points. Then move the stake closer or farther away to create the tighter or longer curve you want.

Set the stake, pull the string tight, and sprinkle a lime path on the ground as you move along the curve. Lime is useful for any ground layout, although a tight string is sufficient for a straight wall. The lime shows up well on grass, leaves, clay — anything but snow.

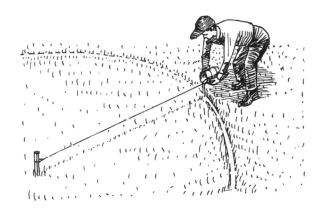

2. After the trench is dug, the procedure for a curved wall is largely the same as for a straight one. One difference is that with a really tight curve, you cannot use very long, horizontally laid stones (unless, of course, these curve, too). As long as you keep the faces vertical, the curve will remain the same all the way up.

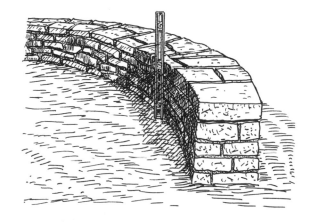

Arches were developed because even a heavy lintel stone will eventually crack under load, as in this doorway to a now roofless barn in Scotland.

Arched Openings

Another excellent architectural touch for stone walls is to incorporate arches. Invented by the Romans, the arch allows a curved opening that is self-supporting. Eventually, even heavy lintels, such as those used by the Mayans and the Greeks to span openings, usually fail because of the constant load. An arch redirects the load and distributes it so that no single stone must bear all the weight.

Arched openings are not only beautiful, but they also save a lot of stone. A garden wall with arches, while requiring more skill to construct, can be as much air as stone. A wall must necessarily be tall to accommodate people-sized arches, and that — ten feet perhaps — is somewhat intimidating. But if the wall is a series of arches, it will lose its bunker look.

You've probably seen photographs of the Roman aqueducts, those raised waterways that fed ancient towns. They were arched because this design was quicker to build and required less stone. A solid wall would have done as well, but also would have divided up the countryside, like China's Great Wall.

Shaping stones for an arch is demanding work. You lay out the arch based on radii drawn from a hypothetical center point. Then you must find or shape each stone so that all adjoining surfaces (radial edges) conform to the radii. It's usually best to measure out the design on a piece of plywood laid flat, and then to dry-fit the stones to it. I work in pairs from the feet of the arch for symmetry, then shape the radial edges of the keystone

The keystone is set in an arch. Whether mortared or not, the stones are dry-fit first.

(the top stone of the arch) last. If my stones are too thick and the keystone is going to be a sliver, I replace a thick pair of flanking stones with thinner ones.

Part of the stone course I teach at Bear Mountain School involves a demonstration arch. We set stones dry, starting on top of a wall, using a form that we have elevated a fraction of an inch with small wedges of wood or stone. When the keystone is set, I pull the wedges out, then the form, and the arch stays up. Applause, applause.

There's really no mystery to an arch. Think of it as two cantilevered stacks of stone, both trying to tip over. Each supports the other laterally, and the whole carries the vertical load around the opening to the solid base. There is no outward thrust; it's all transferred to straight-down force. Early bridge builders routinely constructed arches dry, using only stone chips to stabilize their work. Even vibrations won't loosen a well-made arch, because it tightens with the load.

However, the stones in an arch must be shaped well, or it will have weak spots. Mortar, along with its holding ability, also distributes stress and fills gaps, which is especially helpful in arches.

When figuring your labor for a wall with openings (arches, windows, doors, fireplaces), count the open spaces as if they were solid. This is because the extra work in facing them will equal at least that of making them solid. Less is more, when it's done right.

This semicircular window set in stone illustrates the strongest arch shape.

An arched window in a mortared wall

MATERIALS

- 1 ton (0.9 t) of stone up to 12 in. (0.3 m) wide, varying thickness and length, with as many square, flat surfaces as possible, for every *18 cu. ft.* (0.5 cu m) of mortared wall
- Concrete: about 1 cu. yd. (0.8 cu m) of ready-mixed concrete for every 30 cu. ft. (0.9 cu m) of wall. If you choose to mix the concrete yourself, you'll need about 1 cu. yd. (0.8 cu m) gravel, ⅔ cu. yd. (0.5 cu m) sand, and 9 sacks Portland cement for every 30 cu. ft. (0.9 cu m) of wall.

- Mortar: 3 sacks Portland cement, 1 sack mason's lime, and 1 ton (0.9 t) sand for every 36–45 cu. ft. (1–1.3 cu m) of wall, water
- An arch form, usually of 2 sheets of ½ in. (13 mm) construction-grade plywood with spacer blocks between, and lengths of 2 x 4s (5 x 10 cm) to be used as temporary braces to hold the arch form in place. Have the exact window on hand, if possible, to make sure the shape you build will be correct.

TOOLS

wheelbarrow
stone chisel
striking hammer
mason's hammer
four-foot level
layout string
tape
hoe
large trowel
⅜ in. (1 cm) pointing tool
wire brushes
jigsaw
claw hammer
wood screws
nails

An arched window in a wall is a natural shape. It does not require a lintel as would a square or rectangular window, to hold the stone above it. Since the arch shape is self-supporting, the temporary form can be removed as soon as the arch is completed. An arched window gives a historic feel to a structure, given its association with castles and other early building in stone. This is one of our more complicated projects and assumes you are already familiar with the instructions for building a basic mortared wall (see pages 74–76).

1. We'll assume the window will have vertical walls and an arched top. Build the wall, using the level to keep it plumb. Make the opening the size of the window manufacturer's "rough opening" specification.

If you have not acquired the window beforehand, or if it is to be custom-made, lay out the arch form using a large compass or a pencil tied to a pivoting string. The curve is entirely a matter of preference, from a maximum semicircle to a minimum of just over flat. Locate the pivot (I use a nail driven into a flat surface) and arrive at the proper length of string by trial and error. For a semicircle, you simply locate the pivot halfway between the wall dimensions at the level where the arch begins. Tie the pencil onto the string at this radius and scribe the arch. For flatter arches, move the pivot down — away from the curve — lengthening the string until the arch curve is right.

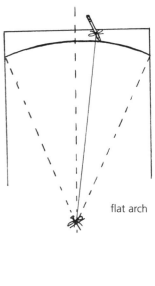

flat arch

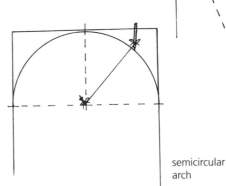

semicircular arch

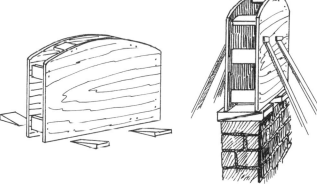

2. Cut the plywood with the jigsaw, and use 1 piece as the pattern for the other. Sandwich 2 x 4 (5 x 10 cm) pieces on edge between. Nail them in place. Allow ½ in. (13 mm) of space here, so the form can be wedged up for easy removal later. Set and brace the arch form.

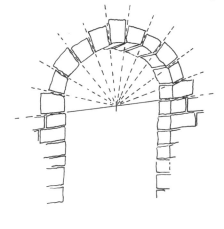

3. Begin laying the arch up with pairs of stones laid from each side. These should be shaped with a taper so that the joints form radial lines to the same point from which you pivoted the layout string. Fit the stones dry, using wedges where necessary. The space at center, top, is for the keystone. This can be taller than its neighbors, or it may be the same size. It should be symmetrical, however, and carefully shaped.

Allow a little space for mortar between the arch stones. The irregular surfaces of the stones will create some space even when they're tight together. If you've built with a ½ in. (13 mm) mortar joint, keep it tight here. If you've built with a wider joint, use it here, too.

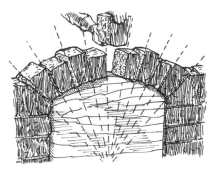

4. After you have dry-fitted the arch, take it apart and coat each mating surface with mortar. Then replace the stones in pairs, all the way up to the keystone. Rake out the joints, clean off excess mortar, and keep wet for at least 2 days.

5. You can remove the form after 2 days, or leave it in until the wall is complete. After removing it, you'll want to "point up" spaces around where the stones rested on the form. Do this with the pointing tool, pushing mortar off the trowel into the cracks. Keep this mortar wet, too, afterward.

6. Before you set the window in place, drive some wood screws into the outside of the frame to extend into spaces between the stones. Set the window, then push mortar into the spaces around it. The screws will hold the window in place after the mortar hardens.

Stone Piers

These stand-alone stone piers illustrate good corner rocks and capstones.

A stone pier, useful for holding up corners of a cabin or a porch, is a deceptively involved little stone wall of its own. It must have a wide footing or it will get pushed into the ground. It must have some mass, or it will look spindly and foolish. And it's got all those corners. Even though piers look simple, you'll spend a lot of time on them. Masons usually charge a higher square-foot price for piers and chimneys because there's no way you can lay them up as fast as you can a long wall.

A five-foot-tall pier for a raised porch should be at least one by two feet to give some appearance of strength. In addition to a good top and bottom, for a pier of these proportions each stone should have at least two good faces, usually at right angles to each other. For the top course, you'll need corner rocks with three good faces.

Maybe you'll set two cornerstones and have room for just one less-perfect stone in the middle on one course. To avoid running joints in the next course, you'll need two larger (or maybe four smaller) rocks. We usually make an end pier L-shaped, or, in effect, turn a corner, for both strength and appearance. That way you can hide some less-than-perfect work back where it won't show.

Stone Piers

Porch support piers, 24 in. (0.6 m) square

MATERIALS
- Stone with a high percentage of square corners — about 1 ton (0.9 t) of stone for each pier 48 in. (1.2 m) high
- Concrete: 1–2 sacks Portland cement, 100–200 lbs. (45–90 kg) sand, 300–600 lbs. (140–270 kg) gravel for each pier footing, water
- Mortar: 2 sacks Portland cement, ⅔ sack lime, 500 lbs. (230 kg) sand per pier, water

TOOLS
shovel
wheelbarrow
hoe
trowel
wire brush
pointing tool
four-foot level
stone chisel
hammer
string
2 stakes

Stone piers can be used, where building codes allow, to hold up a porch or an entire house. Although a continuous foundation is preferable and generally required by code, piers are often acceptable as support for nondwellings. Stone piers require less stone than continuous walls and allow air to circulate under the structure. Unfortunately, the exacting requirements of piers, with so many corners and exposed surfaces, often take as much time as continuous foundations.

1. Dig a footing twice the square footage of the pier. For this 24 in. (0.6 m) square pier, your footing would be 2 ft. 10 in. (0.9 m) square. Dig to below frost line.

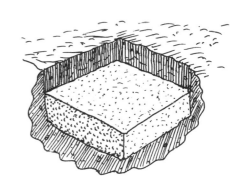

Fill the footing hole at least 6 in. (15 cm) deep with concrete. Start with 2 shovels of cement, 4 of sand, and 6 of gravel, plus water (see "Mixing Concrete," page 65). Mix additional batches as needed. You may want to use more concrete so that less stone will be needed. (If so, you'll need proportionately more cement, sand, and gravel than has been listed under "Materials.")

2. Two days after pouring, begin laying stone. To mix mortar, begin with 9 shovels of sand, 2 of cement, and 1 of lime, plus water (see "Mixing Mortar for Stonework," page 71). Set corners first, then fill the spaces between. Watch out for running joints, however. That usually means laying out one corner with a wide stone, then using a narrower one above it on the next course. For instance, if your first course has a 12 in. (0.3 m) square at one corner, another 12 in. square at the opposite, with two 6 in. (15 cm) squares for the other two corners, you'd have a 6 in. gap in each face. Allowing for ½ in. (13 mm) of mortar, six stones 5 in. (13 cm) square would fit here (one to complete each face; two, with a little extra mortar, to fill the interior gaps).

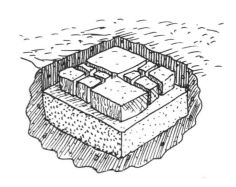

3. For the next course, change this formula so that no joint comes right over the one under it. Obviously, you'd stay away from 12 in. and 6 in. stones for this reason. Instead, use 9 in. (0.2 m) and 15 in. (0.4 m) stones — or, if you have them, full 24 in. (0.6 m) stones would be ideal.

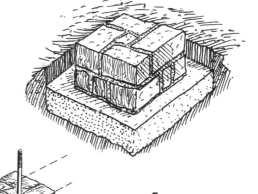

Use the four-foot level to keep the pier plumb. As you approach the top, use thicker or thinner stones to come out even.

4. Usually you'll set an anchor bolt into the pier to attach the porch sill. These L-shaped bolts come in all lengths, and should be set at least 4 in. (10 cm) into the masonry, with enough protruding to reach through the sill.

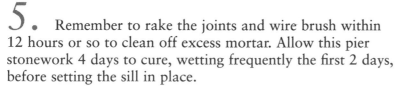

5. Remember to rake the joints and wire brush within 12 hours or so to clean off excess mortar. Allow this pier stonework 4 days to cure, wetting frequently the first 2 days, before setting the sill in place.

Assuming you'll need four piers to support your porch, use the stakes and layout string to keep the piers in line. Do the two end piers first and you won't need the stakes — just stretch the string between the piers.

This stepped dry-stack retaining wall at Thomas Jefferson's Monticello separates the vegetable gardens above from the orchards below. Ten feet tall and a thousand feet long, the wall is benched at the four-foot level, creating a structure stronger than if it had been a single vertical plane. Originally built by slaves, the wall was restored by master stonemason Shelton Sprouse in 1982.

CHAPTER 7

Retaining Walls

HOLDING A HILL IN PLACE may be necessary when you're trying to create a level stretch of ground. To accomplish this requires building a retaining wall, and nothing is as picturesque as stone for the purpose. The level area you create may help turn a previously unused piece of land into a small yard, garden, or building site.

Drystone Retaining Walls

Drystone was used for retaining walls for centuries. The principle is that stacked rocks, because of friction, will hold a certain degree of lateral push before they slide off each other or, because of gravity, before they tip over. With a little human intervention, the resulting wall should provide even greater resistance to slipping and tipping.

Since the bank of dirt you want to hold in place is pushing against your wall, build it so that it pushes back. Lean the wall into the bank by stepping each stone farther inward as you build upward. Or, if you want a vertical face to your wall, use narrower stones — start with about twelve-inch ones — at the bottom and then widen them into the bank as you build. Most drystone retaining walls have a little slope, or rake, to them. They look vertical, but they're fudged a bit to lean into the hill.

All the requirements for building a wall are even more critical in a retaining wall because it is under constant pressure from the side. Any running joints here would allow a section of wall to bulge, push apart, and generally spoil your picnic. Each stone must be locked to its neighbor as tightly as possible, using only friction and gravity.

Against a cut bank, you can build right up to the dirt, without filling much. This holds better, since the bank is already packed soil. Fill and tamp so that the dirt is tight to the wall, taking care not to leave any spaces back there, or the bank will start to wash away.

If you have a long slope or a pile of loose fill, the soil will be harder to hold. Build the wall, stepping the stones against the soil, and add fill with each stone, tamping and/or watering as you go. Water packs soil well if you don't get it too wet.

Dirt will tend to wash through your drystone retaining wall, but if you have laid it tight, the small openings will soon plug themselves with bits of grass, stone chips, and leaves. Growing things will sprout there, too, of either nature's choosing or your own.

Keep the top surfaces of your stones level so that the next course fits well. Most masons prefer to keep the best flat face up for a good base. Wedging and shimming are necessary here to keep the stones from wobbling. You can also fill gaps with dirt, but remember that it might all wash out unless you pack it tightly behind the wall.

The natural slope, where soil will tend to stabilize and pack itself, is a 1.5 to 1 ratio, or a foot and a half horizontally for every foot vertically. Your wall has to hold the difference between this and whatever slope you're imposing on the face of the bank behind it. Soil isn't fluid, so the outward pressure isn't greater at the bottom. Its weight tends to pack it down low, just as the weight of your stones tends to hold them in place down

This drystone retaining wall has helped create a stable, compact platform for parking.

there. As the wall comes up, leaning more into the bank, it exerts more lateral pressure on the bank up where the dirt is more apt to wash away.

A curved retaining wall, convex against the push of the hill, will hold best. As in a horizontal arch, the pressure is distributed over the whole arc of the wall. A concave wall (one that bulges with the hill's push) won't hold as well; instead of the pressure tightening the stones against each other, it actually loosens them.

Keep trees and large bushes away from your drystone work, or the roots will unstack the wall. A tree's roots spread as far as its branches, so stay back.

Moisture will seep through the drystone wall from the bank it is holding, allowing lichens and moss to grow. This moisture can freeze, of course, and help dismantle the wall. But the deeper you build the wall into the bank, the greater the "insulation" provided by the earth. This means less freezing water, and if the wall is thick, stones are less likely to get pushed out. In central Virginia, I build drystone retaining walls at least two feet thick at the top, often three. Over time, bits of leaves, grass, and humus actually act as additional insulation behind and among the stones.

Even the simplest retaining wall requires careful adherence to basic principles: Running joints are avoided and gaps must be wedged and shimmed.

Mason Eric Bolton digs a base for a partially built drystone retaining wall. No gaps will be left between the wall — which leans into the bank — and the cut bank.

Drystone Retaining Wall

A hillside retaining wall, 36 in. (0.9 m) high, 24 in. (0.6 m) wide, 20 ft. (6 m) long

MATERIALS
- Ledgestone, with flat tops and bottoms, 1 ton (0.9 t) for each 4 ft. (1.2 m) of wall, or 5 tons (4.5 t) for this wall. Stones should be from 12 in. (0.3 m) to 24 in. (0.6 m) wide, of any thickness.

TOOLS

pick

shovel

mattock

pry bar

stone chisel

hammer

stakes

layout string

A drystone retaining wall is cheaper and easier to build than a mortared wall, having no footing or mortared joints. It isn't as strong as a mortared wall, but when built properly, can support a slope. The drystone retaining wall is more natural-looking, especially when built of aged stones rather than those freshly quarried or dug from the ground. Also, moisture seeping from the soil bank held by the wall will allow lichens and moss to grow better on the drystone wall.

1. Dig the slope down to the grade you desire, leaving a cut or vertical face that slopes 12 in. (0.3 m) from the base back to the 24 in. (0.6 m) depth at the top. Also, slope the base of this excavation (the "foundation" for your wall) downhill slightly toward the bank, about 1 in. (2.5 cm) of slope in 12 in. (0.3 m) of front to back. Use the layout string to get the horizontal cut straight.

2. Start the retaining wall with stones 12 in. (0.3 m) deep, set against the earth bank. This layer, or course, can be any height but would typically be around 6 in. (15 cm). Fit the stones so they are tight at the face, and fill any spaces up against the bank with soil, tamping it firmly. This first course is a good place to use stones that have rough faces, since these can be turned down and the soil dug out to fit. Reset the layout string to keep the front faces of the stones even and straight.

3. If your walls goes up- or downhill, step the soil at its base so that each stone will be level.

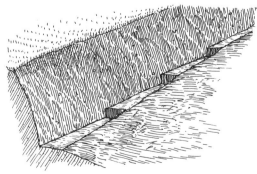

4. The second and succeeding courses of stone should be level and the faces plumb. Use increasingly deeper stones for each level, so that each stone lies on the ones below, with some of it extending onto packed soil at the back. Avoid running joints.

In keeping the face of the wall plumb, you're actually leaning the wall into the hill, holding it in place. Because each stone also slopes slightly into the bank, any frost-induced movement will be countered by gravity.

5. If you don't have individual stones that reach from the face to the bank, you can use two. Use the wide one in front so that the joint is well back in the wall. Don't use a stone less than, say, 10 in. (26 cm) wide (front to back) at the front of the wall, or it can work loose.

Use chips and stone wedges to stabilize loose stones. Pack soil tightly behind as you build, so that rainwater doesn't wash through. Some will, and runoff will eventually plug the spaces with soil, small stone bits, leaves, and silt.

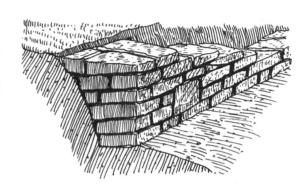

6. The top course — the capstones — should be the full 24 in. (0.6 m) wide (front to back) for stability. Choose these carefully and use wedges of stone to seat these solidly, because they'll get walked on. They can be any thickness, but being large, choose thin ones so you can handle the weight — 2–3 in. (5–8 cm) is about right.

7. If the wall is to slope down at the ends to the ground level, do this in steps, keeping each stone level along the length of the wall. If the wall is to stay high with vertical ends, build a right-angle section at each end, taking the wall back into the slope. Do

this by alternating long stones over short ones to turn the corner and extend the wall back. This creates a buttress that will stabilize the ends of the wall.

Mortared Retaining Walls

If you really want to hold a cut or a fill in place permanently, you must use mortar to seal out water and a footing to avoid frost heaves. Mortar means you don't allow any leaning or shifting; everything must stay rigid.

Where normally a footing is twice the width of the wall that is to be built on it, retaining walls are different. Instead of supporting a heavy vertical load as in a house foundation wall, a retaining wall holds the lateral push of a hillside. The footing here serves only to hold the weight of the wall itself, to distribute this weight so that the wall doesn't settle and crack, and to seal out water to below frost line.

A mortared retaining wall need not be thick to withstand the thrust of a hill, but it should be braced often. To do this, curve the wall into the hill by building in corners and angles or by buttressing the wall.

Especially if your wall will be five feet high or more, it's a good idea to buttress it. Buttresses are simply right-angle extensions from the wall, propping the main wall against the slope it is holding. They get in the way, but they are very effective. The footings for the buttresses must be built at the same time as the main footing so that they can't shift and crack where the buttresses join the main wall. A buttress is built simply by laying stone on the buttress footing, stepping it up to interlock with the main wall.

You can build buttresses into the slope itself, on the bank side of the wall, where they're less efficient but completely out of sight. Back buttresses are stepped to the rear and down, so that the weight of the backfilled bank lies on them.

If you elect to extend buttresses from the front of the wall, they can become ornamental aspects of the work. The spaces between stepped or sloped stone buttresses are sheltered areas that invite all manner of decorative treatment — plantings, pools, seats, sundials, bowers — allowing you to turn a necessity into art.

I don't have a hard formula for spacing buttresses, but the higher the wall, the closer the spacing should be. For example, for a one-foot-thick, five-foot-high wall, I'd build a front buttress (also a foot thick) every eight feet or so. Each should extend about four feet out from this hypothetical five-foot wall. A back buttress holds less, so I'd place one about every five feet along the wall's length.

To hold a slope that will get heavy vehicle traffic, your wall must be proportionately stronger. Consult a structural engineer for specifications, but the bottom line will probably

A front buttress strengthens this mortared retaining wall on a bridge approach.

be a heavy footing reinforced with steel bars, tied into a formed, poured concrete wall with a grid of rebar in it.

Poured concrete and concrete blocks don't necessarily mean "ugly," because they can be veneered with stone for the look you want. We had to do this with the Pleasant Sowell house basement wall when we moved and restored it. The road above carried heavy delivery trucks and the vibrations would eventually have shaken the plumb basement wall and bulged it. Thus, we resorted to concrete.

The front buttress of this retaining wall helps the wall hold back the tree roots and the hillside. While the wall is strong, this is not good-looking work: The mortar is sloppy and too thick and the stones are not well chosen or laid properly.

To hold back a mountainside, this retaining wall incorporates several angles, which act as front buttresses.

Here are a few other tips to keep in mind when you're considering building a mortared retaining wall:

• Mortared retaining walls trap moisture behind them, so you'll need to lay perforated drainpipe back there to carry it off. Backfill with crushed stone over the pipe — that way, water can percolate down and out. Cover this gravel with filter fabric so soil won't erode and plug it, then finish with 6–12 in. (15–30 cm) of topsoil.

• Another way to release water that collects behind walls is to provide weep holes. Set short pieces of one-inch-thick black plastic pipe into the wall to enable the water to come through.

• In place of back or front buttresses, you can strengthen a lwall with little bracing right-angle sections that go back into the hill or out from it. A serpentine wall, too, is strong because it consists of curves, which act much like buttresses. A single curve in the retaining wall strengthens it, especially when the curve is convex facing into the hill.

• Whether you build with drystone or mortar, try to bring the capstones up above the surface of the bank. If it's dry work, the soil won't push the top stone and it will help hold those below. Also, a capstone forms an added lip to hold soil that may wash down the slope and build up.

We formed two evenly spaced buttresses into the bank for this seven-foot-high, twenty-eight-foot-long wall, then brought the wall itself around the back corners, stepping it down with the grade. Of course, we put drainpipe and gravel fill uphill, and the basement stays dry. It was necessary to mortar the stone here, although the original had been dry-laid. The building is open to the public, and busy little hands would not have left loose drystone alone.

The same treatment was necessary for the approaches to a covered bridge we built in Albemarle County, Virginia. Because this structure would have to carry loaded cement trucks, the engineer specified forty-eight-inch-wide footings, a double grid of rebar, and interior buttresses. We used snap ties (steel rods with removable plates at each end) for the plywood forms and left them extended to help tie in the stone veneer later.

I doubt that your first retaining wall will be designed to hold a freeway in place, but you should be aware that using stone for some jobs has limitations.

The concrete of this covered bridge has been reinforced with hundreds of sticks of rebar. Stone veneer covers the concrete walls, which are actually retaining walls.

Mortared Stone Retaining Wall with Front Buttresses

Mortared stone wall, 30 ft. (9 m) long, 24 in. (0.6 m) high, 12 in. (0.3 m) thick to hold a hillside cut

MATERIALS

- 3½ tons (3.2 t) stone up to 12 in. (0.3 m) deep, any length and thickness
- Concrete: 2 yards ready-mixed concrete; thirty-four 8 x 12 x 16 in. (21 x 31 x 41 cm) concrete blocks (optional) to span 30 running feet (9 m) of wall plus 4 buttresses
- Mortar: 1 ton (0.9 t) sand, 4 bags Portland cement, 1½ bags lime, water

- 5 ft. (1.5 m) of 1 in. (2.5 cm) black plastic pipe
- 80 ft. (25 m) of ½ in. (13 mm) rebar

TOOLS

hoe
pick
shovel
mattock
trowel
pointing tool
wire brush
stone chisel
hammer
four-foot level
stakes
layout string

A mortared stone retaining wall with buttresses is the strongest wall you can build of stone. The stones are set in mortar on a concrete footing, and the buttresses act as props against the push of the soil the wall is holding. If buttressing seems too complicated a solution for this retaining wall, make the wall thicker. A 24 in. (0.6 m) thick wall would need probably half as many buttresses as this 12 in. (0.3 m) one, and a 3 ft. (0.9 m) wall, none at all.

1. All mortared walls need concrete footings for support and to seal out water that would freeze and crack them. Dig the footing ditch up against the bank 18 in. (0.5 m) wide and below the frost line, stepping it if the wall goes up- or downhill, as was done for the mortared stone freestanding wall (see page 74). For the buttresses, dig four footing ditches evenly spaced — that is, 6 ft. (1.9 m) apart — 18 in. (0.5 m) wide, 24 in. (0.6 m) out from the main wall on the downhill side.

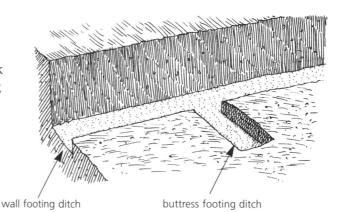

wall footing ditch   buttress footing ditch

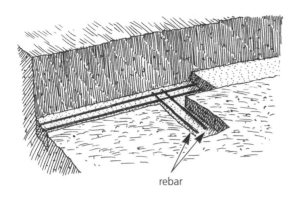

rebar

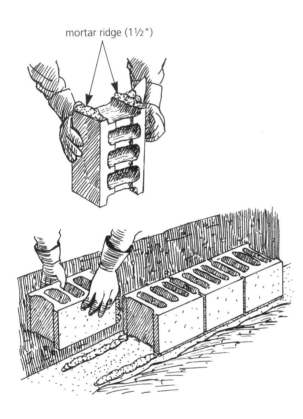

mortar ridge (1½")

2. For this 30 cu. ft. (0.9 cu m) of concrete, I recommend the ready-mix delivered from the concrete company. Just the minimal 8 in. (0.2 m) deep footing would require probably 20 wheelbarrow loads mixed by hand. And if you choose to fill the ditch to ground level, it could require three times that quantity.

Use 2 parallel lines of rebar in a retaining wall footing, spaced evenly in the trench, midway up in the concrete. Tie additional rebar to the long pieces for the buttress footings.

Pour concrete at least 8 in. (0.2 m) deep overall, raking and smoothing the surface of the concrete to a level. Allow 2 days to cure before laying stone.

3. If you've poured a minimal footing, you may want to use concrete blocks up to ground level to save stone. This is always an option and will be strong enough to hold your wall. Concrete block comes in several sizes but 8 x 12 x 16 in. (21 x 31 x 41 cm) is what you would use here. Assuming you dug your trench 16 in. (0.4 m) deep, you'd need one course of blocks, or about 30 of them, for the main wall, plus 4 for buttresses.

Spread about 1 in. (2.5 cm) of masonry mortar — *1 part lime to 1 part Portland cement to 6 parts sand* — on each block. *This is a different mix from the 1:2:9 we use for stone.*

Look for a shallow groove lengthwise down the middle of the block, which tells you this is the bottom. Stand each block on end to "butter" 2 ridges of mortar that will be the vertical joints inside and out to the next block in the course. The mortar ridge will be about 1½ in. (4 cm) high along the inside and outside edges of the ends of the blocks. Then tamp each block into place, leveling as you go.

If you have a lot of rough stones, you can use them belowground, with a lot of mortar to fill out the irregular shapes.

4. Build the wall as you would a freestanding mortared wall (see page 74), but here there is no need to keep the back even. Interlock the buttress stones with the main wall.

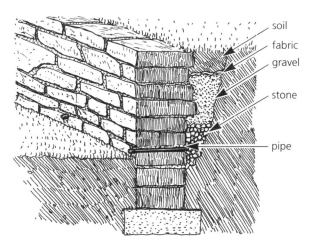

soil
fabric
gravel
stone
pipe

5. Install weep holes so that water from the hillside can come through. I use short pieces of black plastic pipe mortared through the wall. Fill behind it with crushed stone or round creek gravel to allow the water to move easily down through it and into the pipes. Fill behind with gravel at least 1 ft. (0.3 m) deep, then cover with filter fabric, which lets water through but keeps silt out. Then fill with soil to the top of the finished wall.

This sturdy retaining wall in Pennsylvania holds back the earth from the sidewalk.

This multileveled entryway, built with style and precision, combines many shapes and lengths, creating a strong statement.

CHAPTER 8

Entryways

NO OTHER SUBSTANCE makes a more elegant entry to a house or an estate than stone. Passing through a stone approach prepares you for something beyond the ordinary. Whether it's a rustic gateway of natural stones dry-stacked and uneven or a finely laid cut-stone entrance complete with wrought-iron gate, stone says class. One can't help wondering about what lies ahead. If the owners went to this much effort on the entryway, what will the house be like?

Entryways, though, are all too often afterthoughts. When all the money is spent on the house, maybe on some landscaping, entrances are left undone. But first impressions being what they are, you should start making your tasteful statement out front. And if the general public never comes through your entryway, people just may assume you live in a mansion back there in the woods.

Entry Pillars

The simplest entry is a pair of stone pillars, either built up of individual stones or composed of big, one-piece shafts set on end, rising from the ground. Unless you pay for quarried, one-piece stone, you're more apt to choose the built version.

An entry pillar is a simple stone wall, not very long, with a lot of cornerstones. Many pillars are really just stone piers, with perhaps more attention paid to their appearance. Where a pier will often have a back side that is under a porch or building, a pillar can be seen from all sides and therefore needs greater care.

A six-foot-tall pillar should be at least thirty inches square, preferably thirty-six inches, for proportion. It should be mortared, on a footing that extends a foot beyond it on all sides

A farm entrance with beaded cap pillars in Free Union, Virginia was beautifully built of Shenandoah granite.

The dry-stack look gives greater elegance to this entryway pillar, which is joined to a stone wall.

and below the frost line. As with all stonework, avoid running joints, shape corners clearly, and rake joints to let the stones stand out sharply.

You may want your pillar to have a bead near the top — that is, a narrow ledge jutting out on all sides, like those on older chimneys. The bead can be anything that looks good. I like a three-inch-thick bead extending about that distance from the pillar. Then there should be enough stone above it to balance, another four to six inches, say, for that hypothetical six-foot, thirty-inch-square pillar.

It's easiest to lay up the outer stones for such a pillar, paying attention to your corners and checking often to keep it all level. You can use any depth stone that fits, filling spaces in the center with mortar and rubble. This works better than stone veneer over concrete block, which is the approach most masons would take. With solid stone you can use a wider variety of thicknesses and get more strength.

Also, if you want the dry-stack look, here's a good place to get it. Veneered dry-stack is apt to get rainwater in it, which can freeze and pop off your stones. But with a mortar core and thicker stones, the veneering gets a better bonding. For additional strength, extend a piece of rebar a foot up out of the center of the footing to anchor the pillar.

Entry Pillars

A pair of stone entry pillars, 6 ft. (1.8 m) high, 36 in. (0.9 m) square

MATERIALS
- 3 tons (2.7 t) of stone up to 36 in. (0.9 m) long, with many squared corners and flat surfaces
- Concrete: 1 cu. yd. (0.8 cu m) ready-mixed concrete (depending on whether the concrete fills the footing hole to the top of the grade or just

partway). If you choose to mix the concrete yourself you'll need about 1 cu. yd. (0.8 cu m) gravel, ⅔ cu. yd. (0.5 cu m) sand, and 9 sacks Portland cement.
- Mortar: 6 sacks Portland cement, 2 sacks lime, 1½ tons (1.4 t) sand, water

TOOLS
wheelbarrow
hoe
pick
shovel
trowel
pointing tool
wire brush
stone chisel
hammer
four-foot level

Entry pillars require a lot of good cornerstones if they are to look right. Since this project is entirely one for appearance, you should find only the best stones. And while you can shape the ends or edges of stones, shaping the visible corners, which will be so prominent, takes a high degree of skill. Since stonework began, builders have always used the best stones for the corners, filling in with poorer ones.

1. Dig two 48 in. (1.2 m) square footing holes to below frost line. Pour 8–12 in. (0.2–0.3 m) of concrete in each, or fill to grade, which will mean more concrete. If you are mixing the concrete yourself, start with 2 shovels of cement, 4 of sand, and 6 of gravel, plus water (see "Mixing Concrete," page 65).

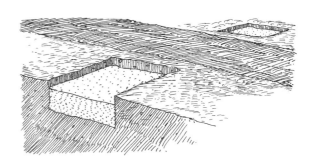

2. To mix mortar, begin with 9 shovels of sand, 2 of cement, and 1 of lime, plus water (see "Mixing Mortar for Stonework," page 71). Lay the best stones around the outside, filling the center with odd-shaped stones, mortar, or concrete. Lay any pattern you want, but the ledge pattern is strongest.

bead

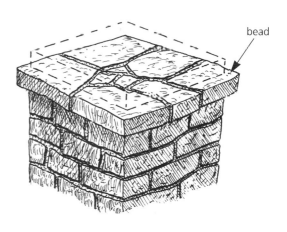

3. You may want to build a bead near the top of each pillar. This is generally about 3 in. (8 cm) thick, and juts out 2–3 in. (5–8 cm) within 4–6 in. (10–15 cm) of the top. Use bead stones deep enough to stay in place as you lay them (the weight of the cantilevered part will need to be offset until you can get more stone on top).

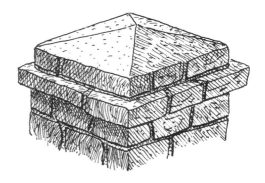

4. At the top, be sure to use mortar liberally; you don't want rain to get into the pillars and freeze. Slope the tops slightly so that they shed water. Keep wet for 2 days.

If you're swinging a gate from a pillar, the pillar must be solid enough to hold the weight. And it's inevitable that someone will bump it with a car, tractor, or truck. You can make the pillar thicker to strengthen it, or you can extend a section of stone wall from it.

One of the most popular treatments is a thick pillar, about thirty-six inches square, joined to a curving stone wall a foot thick, which slopes as it curves, to a smaller pillar. The curve is usually ninety degrees, from one face of one pillar to an adjacent face of the other. Some people like to describe the path of a vehicle turning in, so they make the curve convex. The wall comes out of the front of the large pillar to curve into the side of the smaller one, parallel to the main roadway. Others prefer a concave curve, which cups the entrance area, leaving room for plantings, pools, or rock gardens. Either way, whatever fence is around the property picks up at each smaller pillar.

It would be nice to continue the stone all around the property, but this is an expensive option. When this is done, however, or even if it's extended fifty feet or so, it's a good idea to strengthen the wall with a pillar every eight to ten feet. Of course, the wall must have a footing its entire length. And each pillar is a collection of corners and very demanding to lay.

For gate hardware to be solid, it must be set well into the stonework. Anchor bolts — the lead or plastic kind — set into holes drilled into the mortar aren't usually heavy enough. It's better to mortar in a long, zigzag pintle or eyebolt six inches or so into the pillar as you lay the stone courses up. Either of these will function as the rigid half of the gate hinge. Use at least a three-quarter-inch-thick pintle; rust won't weaken it for a few hundred years.

I've seen round pillared entryways, arches, moon gates, and just gaps in stone walls. The most attractive are always those that appear oldest, with vines or shrubbery obscuring much of the stone. Part of the mystique of stone is age, and it should never look new or temporary.

The high-pillar design of entryways came from a need to brace gates against sagging. A supporting chain could be attached high up on the pillar, or the gate itself could be hinged higher for more leverage against sagging. High pillars, too, could be tied together to stabilize them. A runaway oxcart, for example, could do less damage to yoked pillars than to a single defenseless one.

This gated horse fence runs for half a mile along a Virginia estate.

This iron hinge pintle, set into the mortar of the stone wall, supports a heavy door.

Gate and Stone Wall Attached to Pillar

Pillars at entry, with stone wall and gate

MATERIALS

- 3 tons (2.7 t) of stone up to 36 in. (0.9 m) long, with many squared corners and flat surfaces
- Concrete: 1 cu. yd. (0.8 cu m) ready-mixed concrete (depending on whether the concrete fills the footing hole to the top of the grade or just partway). If you choose to mix the concrete yourself, you'll need about 1 cu. yd. (0.8 cu m) gravel, ⅔ cu. yd. (0.5 cu m) sand, and 9 sacks Portland cement.
- Mortar: 6 sacks Portland cement, 2 sacks lime, 1½ tons (1.4 t) sand, water
- Gate, gate hinges, pintles, and latch hardware of your choice

TOOLS

wheelbarrow
hoe
pick
shovel
trowel
pointing tool
wire brush
stone chisel
hammer
four-foot level

For a pillar to hold a gate and to be attached to a stone wall, you have to build the hardware in and tie the pillar to the wall. Build the pillar and wall at the same time, extending wall stones into the pillar. If the pillar is to adjoin an existing wall, dismantle the end of the wall and rebuild it with the pillar. This project assumes you're already familiar with building a basic mortared wall (see pages 74–76).

1. Having dug and poured your pillar footings, as in the entry pillar project (see pages 98–99), integrate the pillar with the end of the wall so that the stones interlock. Lay wall stones extending into the pillar at least every other course.

interlock pillar and wall

2. The gate hardware is embedded in the stonework as it is built. Pintles can be as simple as steel rods with right-angle bends in them for the hinge loops to sit down on. The latch mechanism, too, can be quite simple, set also into the stonework as it is built. Keep all fresh mortar wet for 2 days.

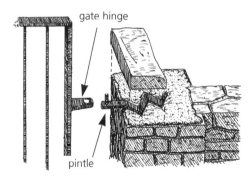

gate hinge

pintle

3. You can retrofit the hardware by drilling into the mortar joints with a masonry bit and using metal anchors. However, setting the hardware in wet mortar as the pillar is built poses fewer problems in the long run, and is stronger.

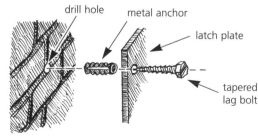

drill hole

metal anchor

latch plate

tapered lag bolt

A high arch was the ultimate in style when the well-to-do were driven about in carriages. There might be an arched opening in a very high wall, a freestanding arch going up from a more reasonable height — six feet, for example — or a four-foot wall that increased in height as it neared the gateway to enclose the arched opening.

Building an arched entryway is a major undertaking: You must build it high enough to accommodate tall vehicles or loads, and it mustn't fall down if bumped. That means a lot of mass up there.

Entryways were traditionally set back from the main road. This allowed the wagon or automobile driver to stop out of traffic to open the gate. It's still a practical idea, even without a gate, because a vehicle needs some room when turning in. And once straightened out again, it should clear each pillar by no less than two feet.

So set pillars at least twelve feet apart. Most cars are only six feet wide, but trucks are up to eight feet. And some fool will eventually back through with his door open. Or if you're in the country, someone will want to bring in a hay rake or paving machine. Be ready for them all.

A moon gate is simply an upright arch that is set upon a mirroring inverted arch. It's designed for people or animals, not wide vehicles. Since most folks are of normal height, a moon gate can be well under eight feet tall (though it has to be strong enough to stay in place if struck by a stray forehead). Usually half its height is above the top of the wall.

I build a moon gate using an arch form as a guide for the inverted lower opening in the wall as I lay it up. Then, at wall height, I wedge up the same form and lay up the arch from both ends. The arch needs stability, so it should be at least a foot thick, and the stones must fit securely. Give the mortar two days to cure, wetting it often, and then remove the form. You'll need to point up gaps where the stones rested on the form, and keep this mortar wet, too.

Rarely is an arched gateway done in dry stone, and I would not advise it. While built for thousands of year this way, it can be done much more safely and solidly using mortar in a mortared wall on a concrete footing.

An unusual pointed arch marks the entryway for a thirteenth-century castle at Fort William, Scotland.

Flattened, unsupported arches like this one are rare. As with all stone arches, however, joints are laid out on radial lines from a central point.

Moon Gate or Arched Entry

Moon gate or arched entryway in a stone wall

MATERIALS

- 1 ton (0.9 t) of stones up to 12 in. (0.3 m) wide, varying in thickness and length, with as many square, flat surfaces as possible, for every *18 cu. ft.* *(0.5 cu m)* of mortared wall.
- Concrete: about 1 cu. yd. (0.8 cu m) of ready-mixed concrete for every 30 cu. ft. (0.9 cu m) of wall. If you choose to mix the concrete yourself, you'll need about 1 cu. yd. (0.8 cu m) gravel, ⅔ cu. yd (0.5 cu m) sand, and 9 sacks

Portland cement for every 30 cu. ft. (0.9 cu m) of wall

- Mortar: 3 sacks Portland cement, 1 sack mason's lime, and 1 ton (0.9 t) of sand for every 36–45 cu. ft. (1.0–1.3 cu m) of wall, water
- An arch form, usually of 2 sheets of ½ in. (13 mm) construction-grade plywood with spacer blocks between, and lengths of 2 x 4s (5 x 10 cm) to be used as temporary braces to hold the arch form in place

TOOLS

wheelbarrow
stone chisel
striking hammer
mason's hammer
four-foot level
tape
layout string
hoe
large trowel
⅜ in. (1 cm) pointing tool
wire brushes
jigsaw
claw hammer
nails

This is a complicated project and assumes that you're already familiar with building a basic mortared wall (see pages 74–76). If the top of the moon gate or the arch is to be incorporated into the wall itself, the wall must be around 7 ft. (2.1 m) high, and can be relatively thin, 12 in. (0.3 m), perhaps. If the top is to rise above the wall, it is structurally better to make your wall and arch, say, 18–24 in. (0.5–0.6 m) thick.

1.

Having built your wall, using the level to keep it plumb, lay out the arch form using a large compass or a pencil tied to a pivoting string. The curve is entirely a matter of preference, from a maximum semicircle to a minimum of just over flat. Locate the pivot (I use a nail driven into a flat surface) and arrive at the proper length of string by trial and error.

For a moon gate or semicircular arch, simply locate the pivot halfway between the wall dimensions at a point where the arch begins. Tie the pencil onto the string at this radius and scribe the arch. For flatter entry arches, move the pivot down — away from the curve — lengthening the string until the arch curve is right.

Cut the plywood with the jigsaw, and use 1 piece as the pattern for the other. Sandwich spacer blocks or 2 x 4 pieces on edge between.

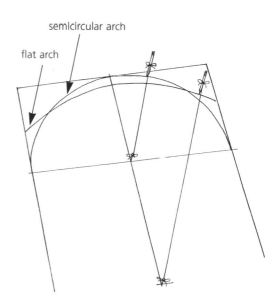

semicircular arch

flat arch

Keep the following points in mind:

- Stones should be shaped with a taper so that the joints form radial lines to the same point from which you pivoted the layout string.

- When dry-fitting the stones, allow a little space for mortar between the arch stones. The irregular surfaces of the stones will create some space even when they are tight together.

- If you've built the wall with a ½ in. (13 mm) mortar joint, keep it tight here. If you've built with a wider joint, use it here, too.

2. For a moon gate, the semicircular arch form is first used with the flat (diameter) side up. Set and brace the form, leaving ½ in. (13 mm) of space between the round edge of the form and the wall, so that the form can be wedged up. (This allows easy removal later.)

For an arched entryway, the project is very similar to the arched window discussed on pages 80–81. Proceed to step 5, below.

3. Build the lower half of the moon gate. Fit the stones dry, using wedges where necessary. Then take apart the arch.

4. Coat each mating surface with mortar. Then replace the stones in pairs, all the way up to the half-circle height. This may or may not be as high as the top of the wall, but it should be 3–3½ ft. (0.9–1.1 m) high and as wide. Rake out the joints, clean off excess mortar, and keep wet for at least 2 days.

Remove the arch form after 2 days. "Point up" the spaces around where the stones rested on the form. Do this with the pointing tool, pushing mortar off the trowel into the cracks. Keep this mortar wet, too, for 2 days.

5. Set the form with the diameter down. Brace the form with 2 x 4s to support the top half of the moon gate or entryway arch.

    Begin laying the arch up with pairs of stones laid from each side. Fit the stones dry, using wedges where necessary. The space at the center, top, is for the keystone. This can be taller than its neighbors, or the same size. It should be symmetrical, though, and carefully shaped. After you've dry-fitted the arch, take it apart.

6. Coat each mating surface with mortar. Then replace the stones in pairs, all the way up to the keystone. Rake out the joints, clean off excess mortar, and keep wet for at least 2 days.

7. Remove the arch form after 2 days. Use the pointing tool to "point up" the spaces around where the stones rested on the form. Keep this mortar wet, too, for 2 days.

Stone steps at Eilean Donan Castle, Scotland, which has stood for more than seven centuries, illustrate flat treads laid over built-up risers, and stone wall railings. These techniques are still emulated by stonemasons today for projects less massive.

CHAPTER 9

Stone Steps

EXPOSED TO THE ELEMENTS, only one kind of step is long lived. The best-preserved wood will last perhaps a generation, brick eventually will disintegrate, and concrete will wear and crumble. Stone wears, too, but at a much slower rate. Walkway steps, porch steps, and stepping stones are best when laid up with the really hard granites. Softer stone will do for outdoor seats, but the abrasion of grit under shoe soles will wear any step.

I have blue-gray stone from Lynchburg, Virginia, in my front steps. One piece was a cut lintel, over eight feet long, from an old factory building. I could get only one, so I used similar stone from the area to piece the other steps. This softer stone would not be able to stand the millions of feet a monument in Washington could, but it will probably last longer than the house.

We did a flagstone walkway a few years ago that would have been too steep without steps. To make the walkway look as if it belonged, we laid it out with the contour of the slope, cutting across in a controlled descent. When a switchback was needed to change direction, we put in a few steps. These curved around plantings that eventually grew into logically placed obstacles.

You can't always wind a path back and forth — the way a cow gets to the top of a hill — unless you have lots of room and want a very long path. So steps at the steep places make sense; they get you to a level where you can do more creative things with the path. They break the pattern, and they flatten what's left of the slope and hold the soil there, too. A path straight up an incline will wash away unless surfaced, and then it is still hard to climb.

These porch steps at the McRaven house feature a long stone that forms the third step up. It came from a factory demolition site. Note the simple, "temporary" railing.

There are some disadvantages to outdoor steps, however. Although you can lead a cow up them, you can't lead one down. It's also hard to ride a bicycle on steps, but after you've slipped in the mud or had your path wash down into the creek, you'll appreciate steps. They're also a great place to sit.

Drystone Steps

You'll remember how we stepped our drystone retaining wall into the hill on the back side, using wider stones as we built it up (see page 89). Drystone steps follow the same principle, but you must leave a level tread or walking surface. Try to find stones long enough for the width of your steps: Three to four feet is normal for walkways; two feet is cozy. It's much easier to lay each step as one piece; whenever possible, get stones a step thick. Eight inches is the maximum building code height but seven is preferable. The depth, or tread, should be at least twelve inches, although sixteen or eighteen is better.

Such rocks are going to be hard to find, so look for really big stones, and cover the extra depth and irregularities with the next step. That means you need stones that are seven inches high or less, with a reasonable front face. Each stone can go as deep as its shape demands, but it should be at least twenty-four inches long.

Ideally, dig out six inches or more below the step area, and fill with crushed stone. That will give you a solid bed for the step stone and let water run off into the ground. Lay the bottom step with just a bit of slope to the front to shed water. Pry it into place with a long tamping bar. You may have to move it once or twice to add or remove gravel to get it leveled.

Now, that was the easy one. Dig back into the slope for the next step and put down a base of crushed rock up to level with the first tread. Working on this slope, you won't be able to use rollers under the stone, so pry it along (also called

Simple stone steps lead from a driveway to a field.

About Steps in General

- Don't build steps down too steep a slope or you'll never get to the bottom in one piece. Cut a path into the face of a hill diagonally, using steps at switchbacks or where they'll get you to a flat place.
- Always allow a way for water to run off your steps without gouging out the soil alongside and under them.
- Don't leave depressions in treads for water to collect in and freeze; tip the stone slightly or chisel a groove to let water out.
- Keep risers a uniform height.
- Keep tree roots away.

"pinching") — preferably with help, for you're dealing with hundreds of pounds here.

Let the front face of this step lip over the first one to leave the desired tread. For some reason, outdoor steps need more tread than the nine inches minimum allowed inside houses. (Inside, you always have a railing to help.) Sixteen inches is comfortable, but twelve inches will do. Raise the gravel a bit for that slope we want, and maneuver the stone into place. It will not sit flat; every drystone fit wobbles, so wedge it wherever needed. Get it to sit on two points on the step under its front face and shift gravel to hold the back.

And so on. Now, you won't find even, seven-inch-thick step stones. You'll find four- and five- and nine-inch ones. So use the nine-inch stone set in the ground for the first step and wedge the others up to height with nice flat stones underneath. Not the best idea, because they'll tend to work out, but you may not have a choice. Eventually grass will sprout in the dirt that collects around the wedges, which will help hold them in.

If you want permanence and absolute immobility, you'll have to dig below frost line and pour a concrete footing for your steps. This will defy most small roots and frost movement, but it's a lot of money to spend. Using a footing and concrete will let you form the steps of concrete or block, to veneer them with thinner stone. This is the usual procedure of most masons.

You may use stone for the risers only, with graveled or dirt treads. It may sound more reasonable to use stone for the tread, but it isn't. A single, vertical stone with its ends set well into the slope will hold the soil like a dam. A flat tread with dirt under will let water undercut it.

A very basic set of stone steps is under construction along a wooded path.

Stone Steps

Stone steps in a path up a slope; 36 in. (0.9 m) wide, 3 steps high

MATERIALS
- ½ ton (0.45 t) stone, with very flat surfaces, square corners, large pieces up to 36 in. (0.9 m) long by 6–7 in. (15–18 cm) thick

TOOLS
mattock
shovel
pry bar
stone chisel
hammer

A three-foot-wide (0.9 m) set of stone steps will fit nicely with most paths and is easy to build. The stones you use must be flat and heavy enough to stay in place under heavy foot traffic. It is very important to wedge stones, if necessary, so they are stable — a rocking stone step is very dangerous. As with flagstones, don't be misled by nice, wide slabs of stone that aren't smooth on top. And remember that only the top surface and leading edge are visible in the finished product.

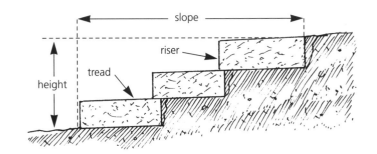

1. First, estimate the slope by measuring its height from a level, allowing 16 in. (0.4 m) for each tread and 6–7 in. (15–18 cm) for each riser.

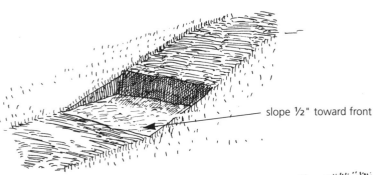

2. Dig into the slope to extend an almost level place back about 18 in. (0.5 m), 36 in. (0.9 m) wide. Let it slope ½ in. (13 mm) down at the front so that the step will shed rainwater. This is for the first, or lowest, step.

3. Now lay wide stones, the full 18 in. (0.5 m) deep — do not piece stones for the depth of the tread. Use no more than two stones across the 36 in. (0.9 m) width of the steps. Smaller stones would tip, rock, settle, and slant. Place the stones rough side down, and dig out for irregularities.

4. Dig back at the height of the top of this step for the next one. Lay these second-step stones (again, no more than two) so as to avoid a running joint. Let the front edges of these stones overlap the backs of the first step stones by an inch or two. Since these back edges will be covered, place the stones so that any rough or uneven edges are here. Shape as necessary, but try to start with good, flat, rectangular stones.

Dig out for step number three, just as you did for the others, then lay the final stones, avoiding running joints. Don't shorten the depth of outdoor treads to meet the slope. Less than 16 in. (0.4 m) is awkward to negotiate.

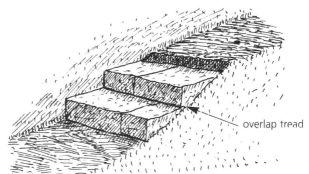

overlap tread

Troubleshooting Height Problems

Stone steps sometimes require you to make adjustments in order to meet the slope at the planned height.

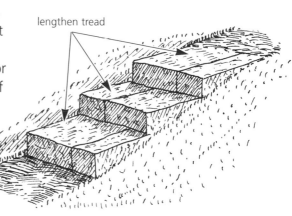

raise path

- If the third step is coming up too high, raise the level of the path above the steps, using the soil you dug out. Pack it, then gravel it, mulch it, or give it whatever treatment the overall path will get.

- Alternatively, reset the step stones, lengthening the tread from 16 in. (41 cm). You've overlapped a little, and you can get an inch (2.5 cm) or so by decreasing the overlap. Lengthening the tread means you'll be digging farther into the slope. If that doesn't bring your third step even with the slope, you may have to use wider (deeper) stones for longer treads, or use shallower risers, say 4–5 in. (10–13 cm) instead of 6–7 in. (15–18 cm).

lengthen tread

- If your third step hasn't reached the top of the slope, you may have to add another step, which will probably require digging out more of the slope than originally planned.

- *Do not shorten the depth of outdoor treads to meet the slope.* Less than 16 in. (0.4 m) is awkward to negotiate.

Get grass started at the ends of treads and risers so that the soil stays put. Grass roots will actually tighten your stones. Bushes look good, too, on slopes next to stone steps. So does a big, mossy stone set partly in the ground.

Nothing makes a flight of stone steps look better than using stone that's already in place. When landscaping or building outdoors, if you can utilize an existing ledge of stone or a big outcropping as one of the steps, you have worked with nature. If this isn't possible, you often can "plant" a big enough slab of native stone and build to it, so that it appears to be part of the landscape. Both techniques are called art.

Sometimes the natural stone doesn't lend itself to a step, but you can work on that. Even a hard granite will respond to enough chiseling for a tread. Or perhaps another stone can be laid up next to it to form a step. Experiment.

And last, sit on steps a lot. They like that.

Porch and House Steps

Porch and house steps of stone are more demanding than dry-stone up a natural slope. At the house, you must get from the ground up to floor level with an independent structure. Thus, your first step has to go the entire depth of the flight to support the others. The ends will be in plain view, too, so you'll need three good faces plus a good top and bottom for each tread.

Stone entry steps lead down from a sidewalk to a flagstone path.

With heavy enough stones, you can piece steps, although it's almost necessary to mortar them to hold them in place if you do. Use the best faces for the visible edges, and fill to level with rubble where the upper steps will cover the work.

Against a porch or house sill, leave one-quarter inch of space so water won't get trapped in there and rot the wood. Wood can get wet without doing any damage as long as it can dry quickly. One of the worst places in old houses we restore is where masonry or concrete has been butted to structural sills. It also makes a superhighway for termites.

By code, porch and house steps must have a railing. Most railings are pretty ugly, so here's where some artistry can be helpful. Iron looks best, but avoid the stamped-out stuff you see on carports and brick rancher steps. It's worth it to seek out a good blacksmith to have something original done. If this is out of your price range, you can set pipe or angle iron in concrete-filled holes in the ground for posts. Bolt on a pressure-treated two-by-four temporarily while you save your money for something nice. When I did this five years ago at our house, Linda chided me, predicting that I'd never get a finished railing forged. Yes, I will. Next year.

Steps up to a doorway must leave a place to stand. Most exterior doors open inward, but you must have a place for your feet while you fumble for the key. If there's a screen door, it'll swing out, so leave a wide top tread. Since you won't be standing next to the door-hinge end of the steps, you can fudge a little here. Exterior doors are usually three feet wide and you need a foot more than that at the latch end. If you want the steps symmetrical, that's five feet wide. Put a potted plant over where you waste that extra space.

When in doubt about how big to make steps, make them bigger. Narrow, steep steps are difficult enough when clearly visible and dry. In rain or ice or darkness, you definitely need room.

Among the most ingenious stone steps I've ever seen are those pictured in a delightful out-of-print book, *The Rock Is My Home,* by Werner Blaser (Zurich: WEMA, 1976). Photographs show exterior steps on stone buildings leading up to lofts. The stones extend from the walls as flat slabs, and each is braced to those under it with a chunk of stone wedged between its outer, leading edge and the back of the one below. Such steps are in my list of projects to build one day.

One thing to remember when building steps in stone is always to keep the risers even in height. A one-quarter-inch variance can cause someone to trip and break something. Treads can vary, but it's better to keep them as even as possible, too. Few people actually look exactly where they place their feet; we have a foolish faith that steps will be equal.

Pennsylvania granite and slate are among the several types of stone used in these steps, which lead from a sidewalk to a landing.

Porch Steps

A three-step flight of mortared porch steps, 48 in. (1.2 m) wide with railings

MATERIALS

- 1 ton (0.9 t) of rectangular stones as near to 6–7 in. (15–18 cm) thick as possible, with square corners
- Concrete: 1–2 sacks Portland cement, 200–300 lbs. (90–140 kg) sand, 500 lbs. (230 kg) 1 in. (2.5 cm) gravel, water

- Mortar: 1–2 sacks Portland cement, 1 bag lime, 200–300 lbs. (90–140 kg) sand, water
- Wood or iron for railing posts, 2 lengths of 2 x 4 (5 x 10 cm) for a railing, and appropriate hardware for mounting the railings

TOOLS

pick
shovel
hoe
trowel
pointing tool
wheelbarrow
four-foot level
stone chisel
hammer
carpenter's tools for making a railing

These house steps of stone will outlast the house, probably. They won't rot or sag, but they will splash rainwater onto the porch or wall, like any other steps. If there is stone in the house, use matching stone here, and try to match the style. Avoid very smooth stones, which will be slippery when wet. And remember to slope the treads slightly so water will run off them.

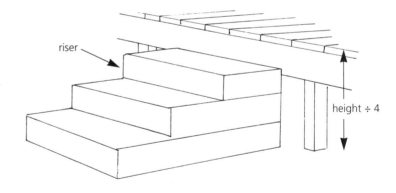

1. First, divide the height of the porch by 4 to determine riser height. The porch will be the final (fourth) step. We'll assume a 6–7 in. (15–18 cm) riser.

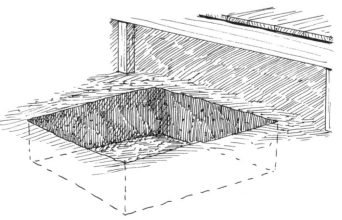

2. Since these steps lead up to a porch, they must be solid and should be mortared instead of dry-laid, so they require a concrete footing. Dig a rectangle to below frost line, the full 48 in. (1.2 m) wide, 48 in. (1.2 m) out from the porch.

3. Mix enough concrete to pour a footing at least 6 in. (15 cm) thick. Start with 2 shovels of cement, 4 of sand, and 6 of gravel, plus water (see "Mixing Concrete," page 65). You'll need about 6 wheelbarrow loads for this footing. You may want to fill the hole to the surface, but that could take three times as much concrete. You can use irregular stones embedded in the wet concrete to make it go further. If so, don't use stones any bigger than half the footing depth, or you'll weaken it. As in other footing work, you can also use concrete blocks.

Let the concrete cure for at least 2 days before you lay block or stone on it. Then bring it up to ground level, if necessary.

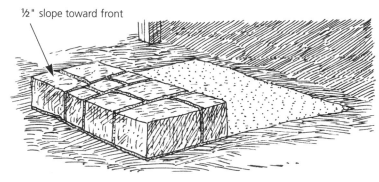

4. Lay the first step using stones a full 6–7 in. (15–18 cm) in height. To mix mortar, begin with 9 shovels of sand, 2 of cement, and 1 of lime, plus water (see "Mixing Mortar for Stonework," page 71).

½" slope toward front

Keep the top surfaces level across the 48 in. (1.2 m) width of the steps, but slope about ½ in. (13 mm) in the 16 in. (0.4 m) tread down to the front. This will shed water. The stones need not be the full depth of the tread; the mortar will hold them in place.

Fill with mortar as needed to create a level surface (side to side) on top. Extend the tread back about 18 in. (0.5 m) so the riser of the next step can overlap it.

5. Now, since the subsequent steps must rest on a base of some sort, it is necessary to build a box of stone, which will be visible on the sides. Extend this first step back the full 48 in. (1.2 m) to even with the porch — as just two narrow walls, say, 6 in. (15 cm) thick. Then extend this wall across the back. Now you have a stone box, with 6 in. (15 cm) walls on the sides and back, and the 18 in. (0.5 m) tread as the front.

You can then fill this box with gravel, broken stones, concrete, or concrete blocks to bring it to first-step level. Gravel would be the simplest material to use, so you might need more than the amount specified — say, half a ton (0.5 t).

6. Lay the next step on this base, overlapping the first tread 1 or 2 inches (2.5–5 cm). Spread mortar on the gravel and on the top surfaces of your side and back walls, and avoid running joints. Recess side and front joints, but leave top ones flush; you don't want someone to catch a heel in one.

7. The third step is simply a repeat of the second, and if you've figured right, the riser to the porch will be the same height as those of your stone steps. Keep stone work ¼ in. (6 mm) away from the wood of the porch so that moisture won't be wicked onto it. (As temperature changes, stone masses "sweat," and moisture is produced.) Keep fresh mortar wet for at least 2 days.

8. Building codes, and commonsense safety, require that porches 30 in. (0.8 m) high or more have railings. This set of steps will have them, too. The rail will attach to the porch post that is part of that railing. At the bottom you'll need posts as well.

For this project, you can use a simple piece of vertical angle iron set into concrete in a hole in the ground. The rail is pressure-treated 2 x 4 (5 x 10 cm). Not pretty, but functional (and temporary). You can set a 6 x 6 in. (15 x 15 cm) or a 4 x 4 in. (10 x 10 cm) post, if you prefer. All sorts of ornamental iron combinations work here, too, most of which are expensive.

9. If your rail has pickets, they may be set into the stone of the treads themselves. This requires drilling with a masonry bit. Then set a lead or plastic anchor into the hole for attaching the picket.

Check with the local building inspector before you plan your railing. Some areas require pickets a maximum of 4 in. (10 cm) apart; others require only the rail.

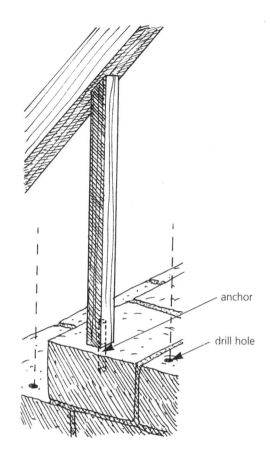

anchor

drill hole

Grouped stones create a focal point in landscaping.

CHAPTER 10

Stone Projects for the Backyard and Beyond

YOU CAN FIND INFINITE uses for stone in landscaping. There are a number of books available on landscaping with stone, but most deal more with design and plantings than with the stone itself. Along with having a good eye for its uses, you must know how to work with stone, how to find the right stones, shape them if necessary, make them look aged, plant them in the ground, get them into place.

Even in areas of limited space, stone can provide visual accent and interest. A friend of mine landscaped her condominium yard — all three feet of it — with a large, mossy granite boulder surrounded by plantings. Another friend placed a single stone in raked gravel.

My first step in landscaping with stone is to design and build around any existing stone. If there is an outcropping or ledge or even a big boulder on the ground, work from that. If not, bring a large rock onto the site just to get you started.

Landscaping with Stone

One of my favorite landscaping projects was in the early 1960s when my friend Jack Cofield had a steep lot carved out for his house in Oxford, Mississippi. One summer, when I was in graduate school, we began to landscape what was a raw, red gouge behind his house. We took a hose up to the top, at a sort of corner, and ran water over the ground. It took a meandering course, along imperceptible benches, to drop off slopes in its natural path. We had to bring in flat stones — there aren't any in most of Mississippi — for ledges that the water would drop

This limestone outcropping forms a natural focus for landscape plantings.

A natural stone grouping around a maple tree offers a focus for additional landscaping.

off. Then Jack built pools below each of these ledges, of ferro-cement (cement reinforced with metal lath).

Jack had spent time in Japan, where he studied the masterful landscapes there. Translating these basic principles to Mississippi red clay took some doing, but it was the natural aspects of what he did that I remember best. At the turnings in the stream, we planted sizable bushes or set large stones. He explained that a stream or a path must have a reason to bend, so we placed the reason there after the fact. These focal points also obscured parts of the stream, so only a short stretch of the moving water was visible at a time.

At our house, I didn't have to create starting points for work we did; they were already there: rocks, trees, a sunken roadway.

A bent maple tree grows from a scattering of huge granite blocks in the woods next to our house. I could not have placed stones as well. It's as if a long-ago giant tree grew in a crack and forced those pieces of the hill apart. Maybe it died, decayed completely, and the maple later grew there, nurtured by the rich organic soil the earlier tree had left. Nice thought.

This tree-and-stone idea has set the pattern for our landscaping. I began by placing a few more big granite pieces

This low drystone wall holds soil to level the McRaven yard.

around the existing tree and stones in order to contain the soil that I had leveled out. That made a nice spot for an outdoor table and chairs. Nothing is level naturally at our site, so we've had to create such places.

Since this area is in dense shade, there's no grass, so we put down a layer of brown pebbles that leads off into a path. Below this small overlook, the path winds around trees to my study, which is of hewn logs, perched on stone piers at the lip of a very steep drop to a stream below. The path, held in place by odd-shaped chunks of granite with moss on them, switches back below the cabin, down the face of the hill.

A natural pool in the creek is accented by a hornbeam tree and trailing cedar. This spot, which has moving water most of the year, is totally shut off from the house activity above. Not much sunlight filters down, so it's cool and quiet. I've begun to build a gazebo here. It's not the place for vines or shrubs, so we'll leave the mountain laurel, dogwoods, redbuds, and ferns.

The yard itself was originally just a long slope, down which an old wagon road had run. To put in a drive without coming straight up — never a good idea — we looped it, skirting an old field under the spreading limbs of bordering oaks. To delineate the yard, we built a low drystone wall and filled behind it with

Flat creekstones, laid over crushed stone with mortared joints, form a poolside patio. The large stone in this photograph is five feet wide and weighs about seven hundred pounds.

black woods dirt. This eighteen-inch wall leveled the space enough that it seems like a yard and shows just enough stone to keep vehicles off. The walk, of brown pebbles, bends from the steps to a break in the wall. Boxwoods my mother rooted and gave us long ago mark the entry.

Up on top, there's a rounded outcropping right next to the house. Attempts to move it have proved that it's the hill itself. Thin soil hasn't let anything grow near this stone, but a huge poplar found a break long ago for its roots. The rest of the yard slopes down from this corner, so it has always suggested flowing water to me. My plan is for a stone pool against this rock, with a stream running off on a looping course around plants and trees in the yard before falling from a low stone wall into another pool at the drive. A small recirculating pump can provide the trickle I want.

A section of the old roadway invited conversion to a pond, and that's where the recirculated landscape stream will end, in a small waterfall to help aerate it. The pond is lined with altheas and a redbud that happened to show up. We've thinned the clump of cedars that grew there to just two. I started a weeping willow below this pool a few years ago. A big round hump of granite at its base gives the area more character and picks up the granite in walls and other accents.

Our swimming pool at the rear of the backyard is surrounded by a creekstone patio in an odd shape that more or less fits the long, keystone-shape of the pool. Water recirculates through the filter system to return as a waterfall over boulders among plantings. This is at the shady end, where the imagination can accept the source of the water.

In landscaping with stone, form can easily follow function. We once had to hold a yard we put in at a house that we had moved and reassembled. The driveway had to sweep in an S-curve to get up the slope, so it was natural to build a drystone retaining wall above it to hold the yard soil. A loop at the top needed some drama at its center, so we planted a fast-growing Kentucky coffee tree. We'd saved other trees at the rear of the site, and these became the beginning of landscaping. A giant weeping willow planted by the owner's grandmother down at a spring branch has provided cuttings for other accent willows. We dug out a boggy place downslope, turned it into a small pond, and placed big stones there to sit on so we could watch the frogs.

Landscaping with stone can mean taking advantage of existing outcroppings, as at this West Virginia rest stop along Route I-81.

Wherever there is something to catch and hold the eye, there should be a place to sit and enjoy it. The simplest stone seats are nothing more than big stones. They get more complicated when they are slabs across stone legs. When a seat is built of several stones, it must have the earth or other stones under it for support. Then it's almost identical to a single step.

Obviously, a stone seat shouldn't have sharp edges or be too rough to sit on. I like creekstones for seats, with their rounded edges suggesting long use, but any "character" stone will do. Avoid stones with dips in the top surface, for they will hold rainwater.

Providing a back to a stone seat usually means building it against a wall. You could set a long slab vertically into the ground for the back, with a second stone against it for the seat. Or you could search for that rare, huge stone with enough height, stability, and the right shape for the back.

An inside corner or curve in a stone wall is one of my favorite locations for a seat. Such an enclosure appears as a destination, a logical place to stop after being led there by the wall. Again, there should be something pleasant to see and experience here. A pool is always appealing. Lacking water, an interesting plant or tree will suffice, or a long view.

This stone bench was built with a single stone as the seat and two stones as uprights during a basic stonebuilding workshop at Endless Mountain Outdoor Retreat.

A simple stone seat is a slab on two legs, set at angles to each other to prevent tipping.

Stone Seat

A stone seat 36 in. (0.9 m) long and 18 in. (0.5 m) wide

MATERIALS
- 1 smooth stone 18 x 36 in. (0.5 x 0.9 m) and at least 4 in. (10 cm) thick. This can be a rectangle or any other elongated shape.
- 2 stones 4–6 in. (10–15 cm) thick and 18 x 18 in. (0.5 x 0.5 m) in length and width. Each should have one straight edge.

TOOLS
mattock
level
trowel
stone chisel
hammer

This stone seat is the simplest to build, being only three stones. The legs will be easy enough to find, but the slab for the seat will take some searching. It must be heavy so as to stay in place, and that'll make it hard to handle — you'll need help or a lifting device. Here's where you want the smoothest stone possible, or sitting will be an ordeal. And slope the top of the stone slightly to shed water, for obvious reasons.

1. Shape stones if necessary so that the large one will sit firmly on the two "legs" when they are set on edge into the ground. Dig a trench about 6 in. (15 cm) deep for each leg and fit any irregular edge down into it. Set both these level, about 24 in. (0.6 m) apart, parallel to each other. Tamp soil tightly around them.

2. Now set the large stone, wedging it if necessary. This is a two-person rock at least, so get help. Avoid seat stones with dips or pockets in them that will hold rainwater. They'll also hold dirt, which will stain clothing.

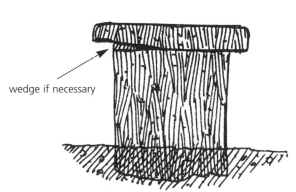

wedge if necessary

Stone Groupings

I like drystone groupings, but be aware that other creatures do, too. Cool recesses are inviting as refuges and shelter for snakes, spiders, and mice as well as the chipmunks and rabbits you might prefer. Some spaces in drystone wall are inevitable, but you can fill between landscape stones with soil.

The principle of a grouping is the same as that of a single accent stone: It should be a point of interest. The grouping can serve as a retaining wall or as the surrounding for a small pool. Above all, any stone grouping should look as natural as possible. You can accomplish this by setting the stones partially in the ground — just laying them on top of the ground looks unnatural — and selecting aged surfaces to begin with. Stones for groupings should be deeply weathered, with lichens and moss, if possible.

Favorite Plantings

Having established a stone grouping, your next step is to select appropriate plantings for it. This is where landscaping books come in handy. Here are a few of my favorite selections, which can compliment buildings and walls as well as landscaping stones:

- **English ivy.** Ivy gives a new wall the appearance of age. It is fast growing and will climb anything. It will also take over and obliterate a wall, so be prepared for some heavy pruning.
- **Climbing roses.** The venerable light pink 'New Dawn,' red 'Paul's Scarlet,' and many of the other ramblers complement a stone wall. Although these older varieties bloom only briefly, we associate them with established gardens. To extend the season, mix in some everblooming roses.
- **Honeysuckle.** In the South, this long-blooming vine will take over a wall. Controlled properly, though, it's a sweet-smelling treatment. Like ivy, honeysuckle is easy to start and grows with alarming speed.
- **Forsythia.** A spray of this spring shrub is a good accent at the end of a wall, whether or not it's in bloom. The arching branches are the right form to hang down over a wall, too, and they provide a focal point at a turning of wall or path.
- **Azaleas.** These beauties are a natural among stones in the forest. Planted around and among accent stones, they can hardly be overused. I particularly like them in groupings of large stones.

Ivy and stone are natural companions. The stonework in this house built by Greg Quinn becomes an element of the landscaping as strongly as any freestanding rockwork.

Stone Grouping

A group of three accent stones for landscaping

MATERIALS
- 3 stones of the same type (granite, sandstone) in varying sizes
- Gravel and/or sand (optional)

TOOLS
mattock
trowel
pry bar
(in some cases) a tractor with a bucket

Stone groupings are so subjective it's difficult to tell how to do them. This is where personal taste is about the only guideline to follow. Certainly the stones should be weathered and porous to encourage the growth of lichens and moss. Above all, they should appear to have occurred naturally in the arrangement you select. Some landscapers set two smaller stones to point or lead to a larger one. Others set three together so they appear to be supporting each other. You should generally avoid stringing the stones out in a line.

1. Dig out enough soil so that the stones, when positioned, will appear natural. The look you want is one of the stones being part of a massive underlayment, with just these tips protruding.

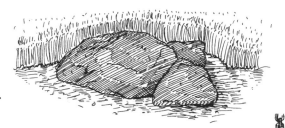

2. Working with big stones is beyond handwork. You may need a tractor with a bucket, or a truck with a boom, to maneuver larger stones. Get a sling around a stone to lift it into place. If it looks wrong, try again. Too much handling will scar stones, and it will be years before these scars age, so use nylon slings instead of chains.

   You can lay the other two around the larger accent stone in any pattern or arrangement. The grouping should be attractive from all visible sides.

3. One arrangement is to surround the grouping with gravel, bordered by small stones (A). Another option is to surround the group with sand (B). Or simply plant the stones in the lawn, so that they are their own focus (C).

   Often a large-stone grouping is the center of a planting of shrubs and flowers. The stones here must be large enough to stand above the shrubbery.

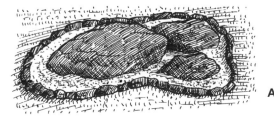

A

B

C

Waterfalls and Small Pools

A waterfall in stone is among the most pleasant focal points you can have in yard or garden landscaping. Locate it in a part of the terrain that would naturally carry water: a dip, a small draw, a dry run between slopes.

It may well be necessary to create the proper surrounding slope for a waterfall, but this isn't difficult. You can move soil with a tractor and rear-mounted blade after it has been loosened with a plow or by hand. Or you can do it eventually with just a wheelbarrow, pick, shovel, and time. The thing to remember is that you need only a slight slope, as long as it looks natural.

Save the topsoil you've removed. When you finish, spread it over the subsoil so that you can get grass started again. The subsoil itself can be used to raise the area adjacent to the swale you're creating. As little as a six-inch cut below grade in the soil and a corresponding buildup above grade can be enough to look like a natural watercourse.

Natural waterfalls are created when eroding water reaches a stone ledge it cannot go around. In flowing over the stone, it reaches the sod below, cuts it down, and lowers the streambed there. The more water that flows over stone, the more soil is removed below it and the higher the waterfall.

In building your own waterfall, follow this procedure exactly. Channel the water with the swale you've dug so that it flows over the stone or stones you set. A wide, flat stone is logical, but

Two waterfalls control runoff from a large farm. An upper dam created a waterfall and large pool, while the lower dam controls the water's entrance into a river.

it also should be thick enough and deep enough that water won't cut under it. For a small waterfall fed by a half-inch pipe of water under low pressure, I'd use a stone two feet wide, six inches or so deep, and eighteen inches back into the slope.

Set this stone level across the watercourse you've created. You can bed the stone solidly in clay or pour a pad of concrete to set it into. The idea is to get the top of this stone level with the streambed above, and dig out below to the depth of the fall you want.

Here it's often more dramatic to dig a pool for the water to fall into. A small stream will make a musical sound if it falls into water. If it trickles down the face of the stone, it's still attractive, but almost silent. More volume will create sound, but that gets expensive.

Your waterfall ledgestone should have a bit of a dip in the top surface to discourage the water from running off the ends and cutting a new channel to one side or the other. It should also overhang a bit at the lip to allow the water to fall instead of seeping down the face. Even a newly cut stone will do here, because the water will soon age it.

Use similar stones around the pool you dig below the fall. I line pools with concrete reinforced with chicken wire or metal lath, letting stones jut into the pool. If these are similar to the ledgestone and other accent stones along the stream, it will all blend nicely. Since we have gray granite, that's what I used with our stream and waterfall.

Run the stream to a logical stopping point, perhaps the edge of the property. Here you need another small pool, with the pickup pipe for a recirculating pump. Screen the pickup to keep out trash and leaves. The best pickup is a screened foot

This combination dam and waterfall turns a simple pool into an artistic statement, while also controlling a stream.

We built this natural-looking waterfall to create a pool, temporarily diverting the stream to construct the three-foot mortared dam wall.

valve like those used in wells. This holds water in the pipe when the pump is turned off, so it doesn't need priming to restart it. Otherwise, you can use black plastic pipe with a piece of screen wired around the end.

The pump can be a simple centrifugal one with a small motor. Very lightweight fountain pumps don't last long; I recommend a motor of at least one-quarter horsepower, with a centrifugal pump on it. Set it somewhere out of the rain, perhaps in a shed or garage.

Bury the pipe to the pump below frost line, or install it so you can easily drain it in freezing weather. The pump, too, must be drained or kept in a heated place. Run more pipe to the starting point of your stream, which again should be in a place that makes sense: a clump of bushes, a stone grouping, another pool resembling a spring — a location you'd expect to see water coming from. This is where the swale would logically begin, and it will be another focal point in your landscaping.

If your pump is in the garage or near an electrical outlet, just plug it in. If not, run UF wire, no. 12 with ground, underground to the house electric panel and attach to a breaker. The motor will require very little current, so it can be on a circuit with outdoor accent lighting or on its own fifteen-amp breaker.

The water will eventually get slimy with spores, pollen, dust, and leaves. A simple cartridge filter will help. You can add a little chlorine, too, but go light on this. To look natural, your stream should not be lined, so water will soak into the ground. Too much chlorine will kill plants. Or you can drain the stream and clean it out as needed.

You will need to add water as it soaks away and evaporates, but this is part of watering your plants. Lining the pools will keep them from caving in and becoming muddy. Plants and grass should grow to the lips of the pools to camouflage the cement. Also, when adding water, the lining will keep the water clear, and the hose water won't erode the sides.

Avoid the common philosophy that more is better. I know of landscape waterfalls with huge flows, and I am reminded of burst pipes. While a spectacular fall of twenty feet or more needs volume, few of us have the environment for it.

In nature, a lot of water carves out a large streambed, and if there are stone ledges, it creates bigger waterfalls. A small stream creates on a smaller scale. What we're doing here is the reverse of the natural process; we're using or building a watercourse, building the waterfall, *then* adding the water. And since it costs money to waste water, we're reusing it.

If a waterfall is a more elaborate project than you want to undertake, instead try making a small garden pool, such as the one that follows.

A well-planned stone pool, with or without a waterfall, doesn't have to be a difficult undertaking to be an impressive achievement. Mason Clay Jenkins built this small pool for the amateur to study.

Waterfall

An 18 in. (0.5 m) waterfall into a 36 in. (0.9 m) pool along a 50 ft. (15 m) watercourse

MATERIALS

- 1 good, flat flagstone 36 in. (0.9 m) long by 18 in. (0.5 m) or so wide
- 5 sheets 2 x 8 ft. (0.6 x 2.4 m) galvanized metal lath
- Roll of safety wire
- Mortar: 2 sacks Portland cement, 1 sack lime, 500 lbs. (230 kg) sand, water

- ⅛ to ¼ hp electric pump
- 100 ft. (30.5 m) roll of ½ in. (13 mm) black plastic pipe, fittings
- electric wire, wire fittings
- filter
- foot valve

TOOLS

pick
shovel
mattock
wheelbarrow
rake
hoe
trowel
tin snips
pry bar
pliers
screwdriver
electrical tools

This project looks more complicated than it actually is. Done a step at a time, it will be manageable. One of the disappointments waterfall builders encounter is the tendency of the water to slide down the front of the stone and run back under it instead of falling free. Slope the stone somewhat, and jut it out so that even a minimal flow of water will fall musically. Regulating the flow a little will also help here, which can be accomplished by installing a valve in the recirculating pipe and adjusting for best effects.

1. Dig a watercourse, following a downhill path bending around logical obstacles, such as plants, stone groupings, trees. A depth of 6 in. (15 cm) is enough if you can make it appear natural; obviously, it shouldn't be on a ridgetop.

Dig out a hole roughly 3 ft. (0.9 m) in diameter and 24 in. (0.6 m) deep in the watercourse. (The hole need not be round — try any shape you like.) This should be at a natural drop in the slope, so the watercourse can continue from the lower level. Dig another pool, any size, at the end of the watercourse; this will be the location for the recirculating pump's pickup pipe.

2. Cut and wire together what amounts to a wire basket of the metal lath to fit into the hole. No matter what shape you use, make the pieces fit together tightly, with an overlap of at least 2 in. (5 cm). Check to see that the "basket" fits into the hole with about ½ in. (13 mm) of space around it.

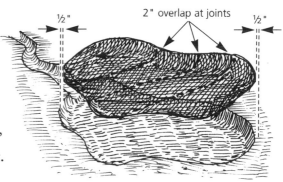

½"   2" overlap at joints   ½"

3. To mix mortar, begin with 9 shovels of sand, 2 of cement, and 1 of lime, plus water (see "Mixing Mortar for Stonework," page 71), for a stiff mix. Trowel this around the inside of the hole, about 1 in. (2.5 cm) thick. If the soil is loose, wet it and pack it into place first.

    Set the "basket" into the hole, pressing it into the mortar. Tamp it, if necessary, allowing mortar to come through the mesh.

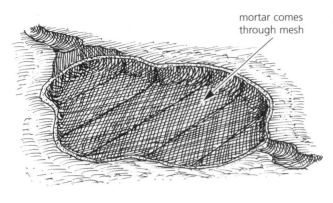

mortar comes through mesh

4. Now trowel another ¾ in. (2 cm) or so of mortar around the inside of the basket. If the lath moves, keep adding mortar. Or leave it for 20 minutes, and it will get more solid so that you can finish. Smooth the inside surface, making sure no wire pattern shows. (If you can see the wire, the mortar is too thin.)

    When the mortar is solid enough not to run, in about 3 hours, begin wetting with a fine spray of water. Keep it wet for 2 days, covering with plastic to retain moisture.

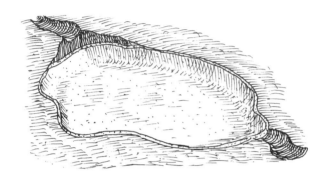

5. The lip of the pool you've just built should be level with the bed of the watercourse downhill from it. Uphill, there will be the bank left from your digging. It should be roughly vertical. If the slope hasn't left a vertical bank, build one by laying up what amounts to a short dry-stack retaining wall across the watercourse above the pool. Either way, you'll now have a small terrace, or step in the slope, with the pool below.

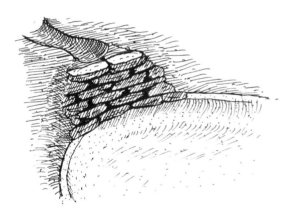

6. Set the flagstone slab across the watercourse, supported by the bank or by the stone retaining wall you've built. Let the edge of this stone jut out about 3 in. (8 cm) over the lip of the pool below. Set this stone level laterally; this way, water won't run to the side and undercut it. But slope it a little downstream to let water fall off the lip. Try to find a stone with a sag or dip in it. Set it into the ground so that it is a fraction of an inch below the bottom of the stream above, and pack soil or clay around it to prevent water from running under it. You can set it in mortar to seal it better.

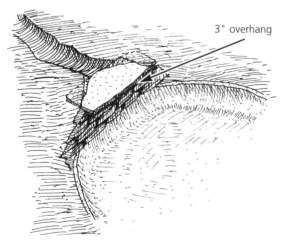

3" overhang

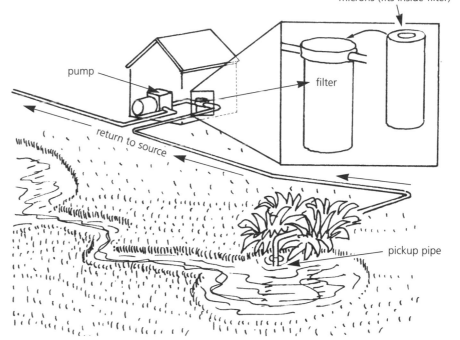

filter element 5 or 20 microns (fits inside filter)

pump

filter

return to source

pickup pipe

7. Dig and build the pool at the end of the stream so that the water flows directly into it, or you could even build another waterfall. You can just let the pickup pipe hang down into it, disguised by shrubbery.

Bury the water pickup pipe from the end pool to wherever the pump is (preferably in a shed or garage), and from there to the starting point of the watercourse. Conceal the pipe in accent stones or plantings to make it look like a natural spring.

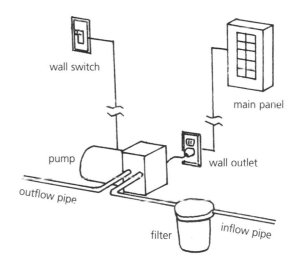

wall switch

main panel

pump

wall outlet

outflow pipe

filter

inflow pipe

8. Install a filter in the pickup line to keep silt out of the system. Wire the pump to a switch, or plug it into an electrical outlet. You may want to run wire directly to the main electric panel in your house and connect to a breaker.

9. Connect a foot valve to the pickup pipe so that the pipe stays full when the pump is off, and the pump won't lose its prime.

Rake soil along the stream and around the pools, and plant some grass. Wait until the grass is well established before starting the waterfall and stream, to lessen dirt and silt runoff.

Fill the pools and start the pump. As the pickup lowers the level of the pool, fill it all the way. When the stream has run a few hours, water soaking into the soil along it will reach an equilibrium, and you'll need to add water only every few days. You'll have to change the filter several times before the stream banks stabilize and the water runs clear.

foot valve

A 48 in. (1.2 m) round pool, 24 in. (0.6 m) deep, curbed in stone

MATERIALS

- About 25 fieldstones, some-what wedge shaped, 6 in. (15 cm) long and wide, 4–6 in. (10–15 cm) high
- Mortar: 1 sack Portland cement, ½ sack lime, 400 lbs. (180 kg) sand, water
- 1,000 lbs. (0.5 t) gravel
- 3 sheets metal lath, each 2 x 8 ft. (0.6 x 2.4 m)

TOOLS

pick
shovel
wheelbarrow
tin snips
hoe
trowel

A small pool can be a simple addition to a garden. Add a recirculating pump for aeration if you'd like minnows or other creatures to inhabit it. The pool is relatively maintenance-free; leaves can be raked out and the water siphoned or scooped out for cleaning.

1. Dig the pool to a depth 3 in. (8 cm) deeper than the finished pool will be, making sure you're below the frost line. Make the diameter of the hole 5 ft. (1.5 m). Let the bottom curve up to form the sides. Line the entire bowl with 6 in. (15 cm) of 1 in. (2.5 cm) gravel.

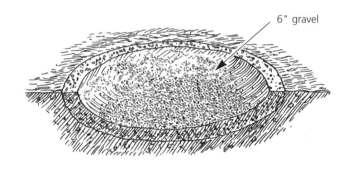

6" gravel

2. To mix mortar, begin with 9 shovels of sand, 2 of cement, and 1 of lime, plus water (see "Mixing Mortar for Stonework," page 71). Trowel it to a thickness of 1½ in. (4 cm).

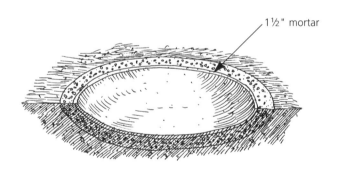

1½" mortar

3. Cut pie-shaped pieces of metal lath with tin snips; you may have to wire the pieces together to keep them flat. Press the lath into the mortar, overlapping the pieces by at least 2 in. (5 cm).

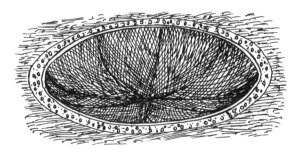

4. Trowel 1½ in. (4 cm) of mortar over the lath and smooth it out. Make sure the lath is fully covered in mortar. Dampen, cover the mortar with plastic sheeting, and let the mortar cure for 4 days.

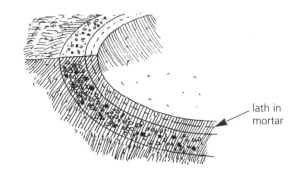

lath in mortar

5. Tightly lay shaped fieldstones around the edges of the pool, using no mortar. (Freezing ground will cause the fieldstones to shift, but not greatly since precipitation will drain down between them and through the gravel.) Backfill the spaces between the stones with soil, and then fill the pool to 1 in. (2.5 cm) or so below the rim.

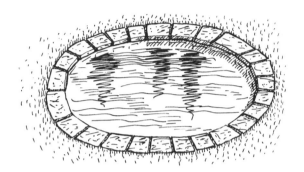

Paths and Walkways

Paths and walkways are another way to use stone creatively when landscaping. Flagstone pathways are my favorite. Brick is formal. Cut slates and tiles are too. Gravel is nice but must be constantly maintained to keep it clear of grass, and it needs replenishing when it sinks into the ground. Also, unless edged, gravel tends to lose its boundaries to grass and plants.

Flagstone is simply natural stone in flat pieces set on the ground. It's best to set it on a layer of gravel down to the frost line (eighteen inches in Virginia); water can drain, then, and not freeze. Flagstone can be set on concrete, but that's an expense not usually justifiable. Be aware, however, that as with other dry-stone construction, flagstone can freeze and buckle and resettle even when laid on a gravel bed. Tree roots are another hazard, for they can buckle even flagstone that has been laid on concrete.

There are three basic flagstone-laying methods: closely matched joints with sand in between; mortared or grouted joints; and stones separated with gravel, sand, or grass for a stepping-stone look.

You can buy square- or rectangular-cut flagstone by the square foot, but unless you want a formal look, you're better off getting random shapes. Ledge sandstone is a favorite, as is limestone in thin slabs. There is a Pennsylvania bluestone that is also available in brown. It's called slate, but it has more of the characteristics of sandstone.

When laying out your path, make sure it bends around natural features, such as trees, large accent stones, and stone groupings. If your course leads you to a steep place, build steps. Go around hills instead of straight up them. Runoff water eats around flagstones on a straight slope, so try to wind around the slope, gaining elevation slowly. This helps control erosion and is more appealing aesthetically, too.

If you must have a switchback to get up a rise, here is an ideal place for a stone seat or for a low stone wall, because a switchback often needs something to hold the soil. A large accent stone also provides an obvious reason for the path to make this sharp bend.

Once the pathway is laid out, dig away and reserve the topsoil, which can always be used somewhere else. Lay your stones in any pattern you like. Avoid very small pieces, because they will turn underfoot. Shape them, if necessary, to get a relatively tight fit. A one-inch joint is appropriate for either a sand filling or mortar. The sand will eventually sprout grass, which will tighten the joints. The mortar will crack, but it won't go anywhere. If you want noncracking mortar joints, you must dig below frost line and pour a concrete footing to seal out water.

A path should have a reason to bend. In this case, the stones and plantings provide natural features.

For a stepping-stone look, place the stones apart, but be mindful of possible stumbles in the spaces. Fill the joints with a combination of crushed stone and rock dust. You can buy this "crusher run" from the local quarry. It packs tight, which is good for the joints but not good when used as the underlayment.

Vary stone sizes and shapes in your flagstone work. Don't use slick or too smooth stones that will get worse with rain. You may find you need to shape edges for the fit you want. If your stones are thin — less than two inches — you can chip the edges with a mason's stone hammer. If they're thicker, use a stone chisel and heavier striking hammer.

You can use a masonry blade on a hand circular saw and score the flagstone with it before breaking off edges. It's a slow, dusty process, and I don't usually do it, but the control is better. Set the blade to cut only about an eighth of an inch at a pass, then reset it deeper each time. A deep score of three-eighths of an inch on both sides will usually allow a clean break in a two-inch-thick flagstone.

Use a straightedge to get the top surfaces of the flagstones even. If there's a hump at the edge of one, that's a potential stumble: Chisel it off. Try to avoid dips that will hold rainwater.

Stepping-Stones across Water

Stepping-stones across water offer a variation on a theme. Here is where you build to one or more existing flat-topped boulders with irregularly placed stones. In a stream where high water will probably shift your steps, use very large stones. A pool or trickle that stays stable will leave your stone alone.

I find stone in creeks and rivers in western Virginia where floods have tumbled them. Each year big ones shift; sometimes there's a path of natural stepping-stones, more often not. I'll often place a few steps to get out to a naturally set one, just to carry stones over. It's fun, and good practice.

Use rough-surfaced stones in water; these won't get slick. One of my favorite streams is Dry River, west of Harrisonburg, Virginia. There are some sandstone blocks weighing probably twenty tons in one stretch, with ripples in them. These were laid down in lake bottoms a long time ago, and for some reason the sand solidified in ripples that stayed.

Stepping-stones should be wide, and that makes them heavy. The obvious solution is to build up a platform of stones on which to lay a thinner slab. Set them solid, though. A tottering stepping-stone is bad for your reputation.

Across a slope, the path need not be level, and its pitch can drain any dip. Avoid really rough stone — again, people might stumble on it. I imagine that bare feet will use the path, so I use stones that are smooth but not slick.

Since a flagstone walk or path will cost in labor and materials, it may be a good idea to transform it into gravel away from focal points. Here again you'll take away topsoil (about six inches minimum) to give the gravel some depth. Border the gravel path with long, thin stones, set on edge to discourage creeping grass.

A stone path is a permanent feature of your landscaping. It leads to points of harmony and serves to link the features of the whole. But it is also a focus itself, promising secluded havens and its own discoveries.

Set flagstones individually for a path, then fill between them with sand or mortar.

Stepping-stones in gravel create one kind of flagstone path.

Path with Stepping-Stones

Woodland or garden path, 36 in. (0.9 m) wide, 35 ft. (11 m) long, with stone border and stepping-stones

MATERIALS
- 1 ton (0.9 t) fieldstone, as near 6 x 6 in. (15 x 15 cm) as possible, with length 6 in. (15 cm) or longer
- 1 ton (0.9 t) flat, irregular flagstones, each 2 in. (5 cm) or so thick and no smaller than 18 in. (0.5 m) across
- 1 ton (0.9 t) pea gravel, any color you prefer

TOOLS
shovel
mattock
wheelbarrow
trowel
stone chisel
hammer

Stepping-stones give focus to paths. This project will surround the stones with pea-sized gravel to accent them, and the border stones will contain the gravel so it doesn't disappear into grass. Also, the stones give a solid surface to walk on, instead of the gravel, which can shift under foot. Grass will sprout in the gravel, which means you'll need to trim it or apply a herbicide.

1. Lay out your path in any course you like, remembering that turnings should come at natural obstacles (trees, bushes, stone groupings).

2. Dig a trench about 3 in. (8 cm) deep and 6 in. (15 cm) wide along both borders of the path. Spread the soil to even out rough places in the path.

3. Set border stones, shaping where necessary, end to end in the trenches, so that about 3 in. (8 cm) stands out of the ground. Vary lengths, but avoid stones shorter than 6 in. (15 cm); these won't stay in place. Tamp soil around the stones to hold them.

4. Dig out a base for each stepping-stone so that approximately 1 in. (2.5 cm) will stand up from the surface. Leave about 6 in. (15 cm) between stones. I alternate large and medium stones, avoiding any under 18 in. (0.5 m) across but leaving at least 6 in. (15 cm) at the sides of the path. This will create the effect of stone floating in a stream of gravel.

5. Spread 1 in. (2.5 cm) of gravel along the path, sweeping the excess off the stepping-stones. Where you've loosened the soil in digging out roots or stumps and where you've spread loose soil to level it, tamp before graveling. After a few weeks, spots will settle in the path. Add gravel here as needed.

Stone Barbecues

A barbecue built of stone is a rather ambitious project for the beginner, combining techniques learned in mortared wall construction with more advanced ones. Like a stone pillar, a barbecue requires lots of good cornerstones. Like a window opening, the smoke opening on an advanced barbecue requires an arch. The chimney is a hollow pillar of sorts. The suspended concrete fire area requires use of reinforcing materials and forming.

A simple barbecue may be just that — a raised stone platform on which to build the fire, with elevated sides to support the grill. An advanced one, however, is more like a fireplace in a house, in its complexity.

A barbecue must be located in the right place, like any stonework, or it can be an eyesore. Properly built, it becomes a focal point and a center for outdoor activities that blends with plantings and other landscape features.

If there is stone evident either in your house, outbuildings, or yard, use similar stone in the barbecue. Before you build it, light a small fire periodically to see which way the smoke usually goes. Situate the barbecue so the smoke drafts away from the chef. If your barbecue includes a chimney, a good draft will draw the smoke over and into the chimney in any but a strong wind.

Build to a comfortable height. Kitchen appliances are a standard thirty-six inches tall, but you'll want to modify that for your own needs. A slightly higher grill height can mean the difference between an aching back and a good time spent cooking out.

A basic barbecue is a pretty no-frills project. Do start noting features of existing ones for ideas you like. A well-built stone structure will be a work of art in itself, but there are niceties you may want, too. I stow charcoal, kindling, and lighter fluid underneath, but you could opt for nicely arched recesses for storage, a built-in seat for the cook, a pop-out canopy to provide shelter from sun or rain — use your imagination.

The project will probably consume more time than you expect. One summer, ten students and I began a barbecue at the outdoor school where I was teaching. As perhaps a quarter of our practical exercises, we just got the basic three sides up to grill height and the chimney arch built in a week. Next year's class got the chimney half up, and it required a third class to complete it. Allow yourself all summer to build yours in your spare time. By myself, I'd need a full week to build a respectable barbecue with chimney.

Gather the stone first, remembering that you can't have too many good cornerstones. Then get the footing ditch dug and the concrete poured. By then it'll seem as if you've done a lot, and nothing is above ground yet.

When you've completed the fire slab and sides to grill height, you may well decide to stop here. That's fine, and you can always add the chimney later if you've built the basic structure large enough to accommodate it. The barbecue will work fine without the chimney, but the victims of your cooking may get a lot of smoke in their eyes. Besides, finishing it will nag at you.

Building this kind of barbecue requires an understanding of many stone-building techniques: vertical walls, arches, horizontal spans, beading, stepping.

Stone Barbecue

Simple barbecue, 36 x 36 x 36 in. (92 x 92 x 92 cm)

MATERIALS

- Between 1½ and 2 tons (1.4–1.8 t) stone, approximately 6 in. (15 cm) thick, as rectangular as possible
- Concrete: 2–3 sacks Portland cement, 300–400 lbs. (140–180 kg) sand, 500 lbs. (230 kg) gravel, water
- Mortar: 3 sacks Portland cement, 1 sack lime, 600–700 lbs. (270–320 kg) sand, water
- 24 x 30 x ⅝ in. (62 x 77 x 1.6 cm) sheet of plywood and five

2 x 4s (5 x 10 cm), each 30–36 in. (0.8–0.9 m) long, for forms and braces
- 20 ft. (6 m) of ½ in. (13 mm) rebar
- Wire or string to tie a rebar grid together
- A handful of #10 nails
- Wire grill, approximately 24 in. (62 cm) square, but wider if you want to set it on top of the stone walls

TOOLS

pick
shovel
wheelbarrow
hoe
trowel
pointing tool
wire brush
hacksaw
handsaw
hammer

A simple stone barbecue is a three-sided structure with a platform on which to build the fire, and elevated sides for the wire grill. Orient it so that the front faces into the prevailing wind.

1. Dig a footing ditch 12 in. (31 cm) wide in a C-shape, with each side of the C, 42 in. (1.1 m) long. The depth should be below the frost line.

   Mix the footing concrete in a wheelbarrow, with enough water for a mix that will run when worked. Start with 2 shovels of Portland cement, 4 shovels of sand, and 6 shovels of gravel (see "Mixing Concrete," page 65); mix additional batches until you have poured a footing at least 6 in. (15 cm) deep into the ditch. (A deeper footing will require more cement, sand, and gravel than the quantities listed under "Materials.") Keep it damp for at least 2 days, while it cures.

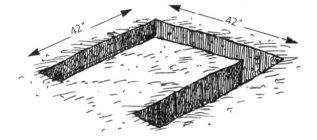

2. To mix mortar, begin with 9 shovels of sand, 2 of cement, and 1 of lime, plus water (see "Mixing Mortar for Stonework," page 71). Begin laying stones, 36 in. (92 cm) to a side; use stones that are 6 in. (15 cm) wide, and center them on the footing. You can use rough stones below grade, or you can substitute concrete blocks. At ground level, build a three-sided wall, 6 in. (15 cm) thick and 30 in. (77 cm) high. Use a stiff mortar mix to set the stones.

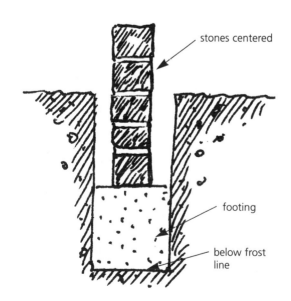

stones centered

footing

below frost line

3. Make a rebar grid. Cut 10 lengths of rebar, 5 of them 26 in. (67 cm) long to overlap the side stone walls by 1 in. (2.5 cm), and 5 of them 24 in. (62 cm) long. Lay out 5 identical lengths of rebar 6 in. (15 cm) apart, then overlay with the other 5 lengths, securing the grid with wire or string. Lay the grid across the walls, with the longer rebar lengths across the side walls. Set the grid far enough back on the rear wall so that you have a couple of inches clearance at the front. (You don't want rebar sticking out of the front of the concrete slab you'll soon be pouring to hold the charcoal.)

4. Cut a piece of plywood roughly 24 in. (62 cm) square and position it 2 in. (5 cm) under the rebar grid, wedging it into place. Use wooden wedges jammed between the edges of the plywood and the stone wall. Also support the plywood with four 2 x 4 (5 x 10 cm) legs, each set in about 4 in. (10 cm) from the edge of the plywood. Nail a fifth 2 x 4 to the front of the plywood to form a lip.

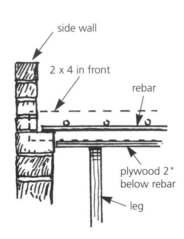

side wall

2 x 4 in front

rebar

plywood 2" below rebar

leg

Add an additional 6 in. (15 cm) of height to the three stone walls, either on top of the rebar ends or set back 1 in. (2.5 cm) so that the walls are 5 in. (13 cm) thick.

5. Mix concrete, as you did for the footing, and pour it 3½–4 in. (9–10 cm) thick over the plywood form. Trowel it smooth, cover it with plastic sheeting, and keep it moist for 4 days.

6. Remove the braces and the plywood, and backfill around the stone walls with soil, if you haven't already done so. The concrete slab is for the charcoal fire. Before using it, spread an inch of sand on the slab to protect it from extreme heat. Depending on the size of your grill, you can either set it on the raised stone sides of the barbecue or support it above the slab using extra wall stones or a few bricks.

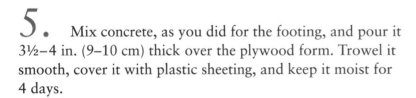

Stone Barbecue with Chimney

Barbecue 36 in. wide by 54 in. deep (92 x 138 cm), with chimney and arched fireplace opening

MATERIALS

- 3–4 tons (2.7–3.6 t) stone, approximately 6 in. (15 cm) thick, as rectangular as possible
- Concrete: 3–4 sacks Portland cement, 750 lbs. (0.3 t) sand, 750 lbs. (0.3 t) gravel, water
- Mortar: 3–4 sacks Portland cement, 2 sacks lime, 750 lbs. (0.3 t) sand, water
- 24 x 48 x ⅝ in. (62 x 122 x 1.6 cm) plywood and five 2 x 4s
- (5 x 10 cm), each 30–36 in. (0.8–0.9 m) long, for forms and braces
- 20 ft. (6 m) of ½ in. (13 mm) rebar
- Wire or string to tie a rebar grid together
- A handful of #10 nails
- Wire grill, approximately 26 in. (67 cm) square

TOOLS

pick
shovel
wheelbarrow
hoe
trowel
pointing tool
wire brush
hacksaw
handsaw
hammer
saber saw or keyhole saw

This is a more advanced design than the preceding project, with more aesthetic appeal. Also, it keeps the smoke out of your eyes. In use, you can facilitate draft by burning a crumpled sheet of paper back in the chimney to heat the air and start it rising.

1. Dig a footing ditch 12 in. (31 cm) wide in a C-shape, with the two sides of the C, 60 in. (1.5 m) long and the back 42 in. (1.1 m) long. The depth should be below the frost line.

Mix the footing concrete in a wheelbarrow, with enough water for a mix that will run when worked. Start with 2 shovels of Portland cement, 4 shovels of sand, and 6 shovels of gravel (see "Mixing Concrete," page 65); mix additional batches until you have poured a footing at least 6 in. (15 cm) deep into the ditch. (A deeper footing will require more cement, sand, and gravel than the quantities listed under "Materials.") Keep it damp for at least 2 days, while it cures.

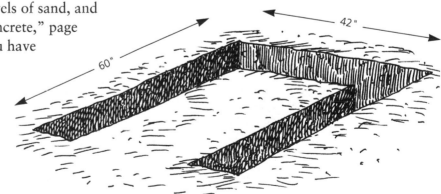

2. To mix mortar, begin with 9 shovels of sand, 2 of cement, and 1 of lime, plus water (see "Mixing Mortar for Stonework," page 71). Begin laying stones, 54 in. (138 cm) to each side and 36 in. (92 cm) to the back; use stones that are 6 in. (15 cm) wide, and center them on the footing. You can use rough stones below grade, or you can substitute concrete blocks. At ground level, build a three-sided wall, 6 in. (15 cm) thick and 30 in. (77 cm) high. Use a stiff mortar mix to set the stones.

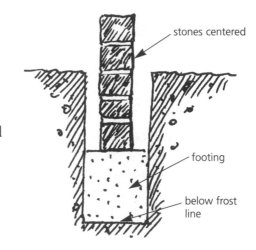

stones centered

footing

below frost line

3. Make a rebar grid. Cut 10 lengths of rebar, 5 of them 26 in. (67 cm) long to overlap the side stone walls by 1 in. (2.5 cm), and 5 of them 24 in. (62 cm) long. Lay out 5 identical lengths of rebar 6 in. (15 cm) apart, then overlay with the other 5 lengths, securing the grid with wire or string. Lay the grid across the walls, with the longer rebar lengths across the side walls. Set the grid far enough back on the rear wall so that you have a couple of inches clearance at the front. (You don't want rebar sticking out of the front of the concrete slab you'll soon be pouring to hold the charcoal.)

4. Cut a piece of plywood roughly 24 in. (62 cm) square and position it 2 in. (5 cm) under the rebar grid, wedging it into place. Use wooden wedges jammed between the edges of the plywood and the stone wall. Also support the plywood with four 2 x 4 (5 x 10 cm) legs, each set in about 4 in. (10 cm) from the edge of the plywood. Nail a fifth 2 x 4 to the front of the plywood to form a lip.

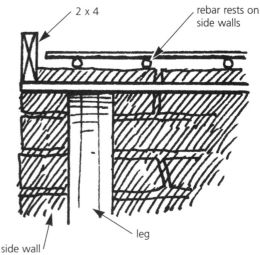

2 x 4

rebar rests on side walls

side wall

leg

5. Add an additional 6 in. (15 cm) of height to the three stone walls before preparing the concrete slab.

Mix concrete, as you did for the footing, and pour it 3½–4 in. (9–10 cm) thick over the plywood form. Trowel it smooth, cover it in plastic, and keep it moist for 4 days, then remove the braces and the plywood. Backfill around the stone walls with soil, if you haven't already done so.

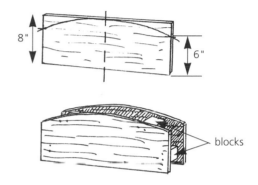

6. Prepare a plywood form for the arch. Make it 24 in. (62 cm) wide and 8 in. (21 cm) high. Beginning 6 in. (15 cm) up the sides, scribe a curve that peaks at 8 in. (21 cm). Cut out the form, then duplicate it on a second piece of plywood. Cut out the second form and nail the two together, separated by 3–4 in. (8–10 cm) wooden blocks.

7. Lay your form on the ground and select and shape pairs of tapered stones to conform to the arch. Dry-fit the stones, allowing ½ in. (13 mm) of space for mortar between them and keeping the joints pointing toward a single focal point.

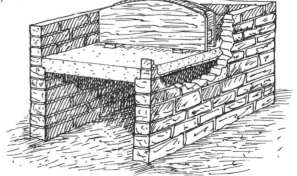

8. Once you have your stones selected, set the form upright on wooden wedges for easy removal later, 30 in. (77 cm) back from the front of the side walls.

9. Begin laying up the arch stones. Start with pairs of tapered stones at each end of the form, keeping the joints pointing to a focal point and coating each side surface with ½ in. (13 mm) of mortar. Continue by placing paired stones up each side of the arch form. Place the keystone last. Remove the arch form a day after you've set the keystone.

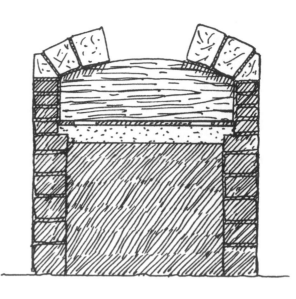

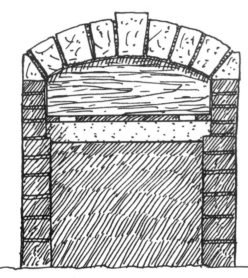

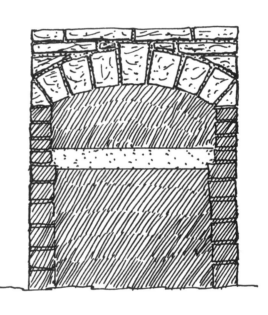

10. Blend the arch stones with more wall stones to a height above the arch. The wedge-shaped arch stones will be irregular in relation to the wall's horizontal stones, so use odd-shaped stone to tie the arch and the rest of the stonework together.

11. Begin stepping in the side walls, 2 in. (5 cm) at a step. You may also step in the front chimney wall. You'll need only 8 in. (21 cm) square or so inside the chimney to carry the smoke, so the degree to which you step in the chimney is up to you.

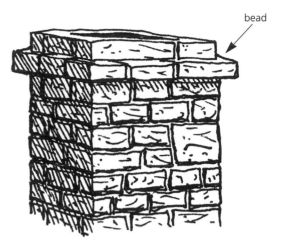
bead

12. Chimney height is optional. Usually 8–12 ft. (2.4–3.6 m) of overall height is proportionate. If you want a bead near the top, as in many older house chimneys, use stones 2–3 in. (5–8 cm) thick that will jut out 2 in. (5 cm), within 6 in. (15 cm) of the top. Use bead stones deep enough to stay in place as you lay them (the weight of the cantilevered part will need to be offset until you can get more stone on top.)

Before using the barbecue, spread an inch of sand on the concrete slab to protect it from extreme heat. Support the wire grill above the slab using extra wall stones or a few bricks.

Birdbaths

A birdbath may seem like an anachronism, but in fact it can be a landscaping focal point. Add a fountain and building one becomes an exercise in elegance. Moreover, when the birdbath is of stone instead of precast concrete or metal, it attains that level of permanence and dignity that characterizes all good stonework. Built of stone natural to the area, it will blend well and be a fitting addition to any lawn. And it *will* attract birds.

Now, building anything with running water is more complicated than simple stone wall work, but a birdbath isn't really that difficult a project. Like all stonework it should be approached a step at a time and not allowed to intimidate.

A very small fountain pump will suffice. Water is being moved in such a small volume for so short a distance that a large pump is a waste. You may want just a bubbling effect or a small geyser. Either way, not much force is necessary. A larger flow or more pressure will send the water up high where wind will scatter it, and the birdbath will soon go dry.

Do keep an eye on the water level, since the pump will burn out if it runs dry. Evaporation will, of course, lessen the reserve, and birds splash out a lot. Any recirculating water feature should be checked daily and the water level maintained.

Birdbath with Fountain

A circular birdbath with fountain, 48 in. (1.2 m) high and 36 in. (0.9 m) in diameter

MATERIALS

- 2 tons (1.8 t) stone, mostly 6 in. (15 cm) thick, relatively short lengths.Corbeling for the top courses will require stones 8-10 in. (20-25 cm) thick.
- Concrete: 2 sacks Portland cement, 250 lbs. (0.1 t) sand, 500 lbs. (0.2 t) gravel, water
- Mortar: 4 sacks Portland cement, 1½ sacks lime, 750 lbs. (0.3 t) sand, water
- 36 in. (92 cm) square metal lath
- 36 x 36 x ⅝ in. (92 x 92 x 1.6 cm) sheet of plywood and four 2 x 4s (5 x 10 cm), each about 36 in. (0.9 m) long, for form and braces

- 6 ft. (1.8 m) of pressure-treated 2 x 4s (5 x 10 cm) for door frame
- Wood and hardware for door: 15 x 16 x 1 in. (38 x 41 x 2.5 cm) pine or oak board, 2 door hinges, screen door latch or turn block latch, stainless steel screws
- Several ¾ in. (2 cm) wooden dowels, 9 in. (23 cm) long, tapered at one end
- 10 gal. (38 l) plastic water tank, no larger than 14 x 15 in. (36 x 28 cm) wide and high
- Small pump, fittings, adjustable hose nozzle, electric cord
- ½ in. (13 mm) polybutylene pipe, 10 ft. (3 m) long

TOOLS

pick
shovel
wheelbarrow
hoe
trowel
pointing tool
saber saw
hand or circular saw
two pipe wrenches
hammer
tape measure
level
square
marking pencil

A stone birdbath departs from the usual pedestal. Because stone looks better as a mass, this project is a round structure, 48 in. (1.2 m) high, with the basin formed in the top. The base houses a recirculating pump and water storage tank, with a wooden door providing access. The height of the water plume is up to you.

1. Dig a circular footing ditch 12 in. (0.3 m) wide and 42 in. (1.1 m) in diameter (measured from the outer edge of the footing), to below the frost line.

Mix the concrete. Start with 2 shovels of cement, 4 of sand, and 6 of gravel, plus water (see "Mixing Concrete," page 65). Mix additional batches as needed to fill the footing ditch to a depth of at least 6 in. (15 cm). (A deeper footing will require more cement, sand, and gravel than the quantities listed under "Materials.") Keep it damp for at least 2 days.

2. To mix mortar, begin with 9 shovels of sand, 2 of cement, and 1 of lime, plus water (see "Mixing Mortar for Stonework," page 71). Begin laying stone for the wall, which should be 6 in. (15 cm) thick and centered on the footing.

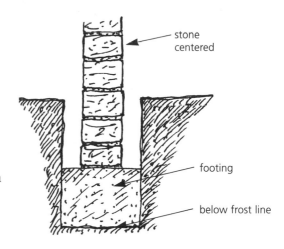

stone centered

footing

below frost line

3. Just above ground level, set the door frame — pieces of pressure-treated 2 x 4 (5 x 10 cm) cut to support a 15 x 16 in. (38 x 41 cm) door. (The curve of the wall will accommodate a straight door if the door is recessed a bit.) Anchor the frame to the stonework with stainless steel screws protruding from the wood so that they can be mortared in.

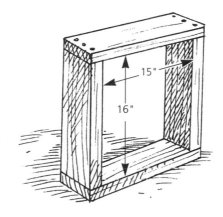

15"

16"

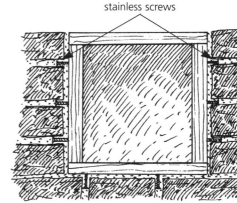

stainless screws

4. Drill a ½ in. (13 mm) hole in the wood for an electric wire, or leave a hole in the mortar by mortaring in a ½ in. (13 mm) dowel that you've tapered so you can remove it easily after the mortar dries. Set the dowel between stones or between stone and frame.

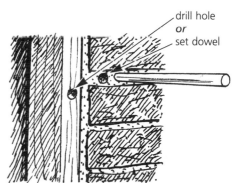

drill hole
or
set dowel

5. Continue the circular wall, measuring often to stay round and plumb. At the top of the door frame, lay a lintel stone, curved if possible.

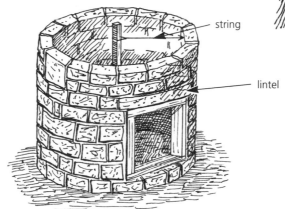

string

lintel

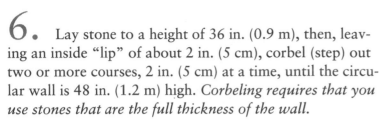

leave lip

6. Lay stone to a height of 36 in. (0.9 m), then, leaving an inside "lip" of about 2 in. (5 cm), corbel (step) out two or more courses, 2 in. (5 cm) at a time, until the circular wall is 48 in. (1.2 m) high. *Corbeling requires that you use stones that are the full thickness of the wall.*

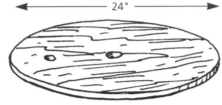

24"

7. Cut a circle of plywood, with a diameter of about 24 in. (0.6 m), to fit inside the wall, 12 in. (0.3 m) below the final height. Cut the circumference of the plywood circle to accommodate unevenness in the stone wall. Drill a ¾ in. (2 cm) hole in the center of the disc, and another 3 in. (8 cm) from the edge.

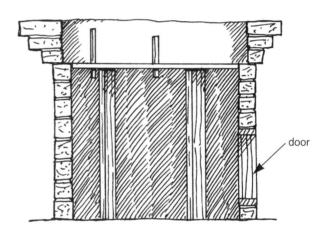

door

8. Fit a tapered 9 in. (23 cm) wooden dowel into each hole, then prop the form up with 2 x 4s (5 x 10 cm) that extend to the ground. Position the circular form so that the hole near the outer edge is as far from the door as possible.

9. Mix additional mortar and trowel it onto the plywood form, shaping it into a curved bowl. The mortar should be fairly stiff to keep it from sliding down the sides.

When the mortar is 1½ in. (4 cm) thick at the bottom of the bowl, cut pie-shaped pieces of metal lath, each about 18 in. (46 cm) from point to arc, and lay them overlapping each other by about 2 in. (5 cm) to fit the curve of the bowl.

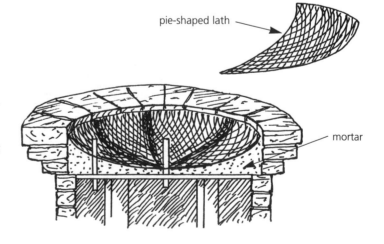

pie-shaped lath

mortar

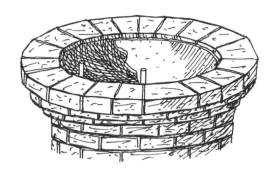

10. Trowel another 1½ in. (4 cm) or so of mortar over the lath, and smooth it out. At what will be water level — say, 2 in. (5 cm) down from the lip of the bowl — the outermost dowel should protrude. (When removed later, this will leave an overflow hole.)

Cover the mortar with plastic sheeting and keep it damp for 4 days. Then remove the plywood form by screwing drywall screws into it and prying downward with a claw hammer or crowbar. It should come off the dowels, which can be driven upward and out with a long punch or another, smaller piece of doweling. Cut the plywood form into pieces with the saber saw to get it out the door space.

11. Now you're ready to put in the pipes. Set the overflow pipe in the side dowel hole, and the nozzle pipe in the center hole then apply mortar around both. Let the mortar cure for 4 days, covered in plastic, and then caulk. Run the overflow pipe down to the tank, which can be set on the ground. Run the nozzle pipe down to the pump. The pickup pipe from the pump should extend to within 1 in. (2.5 cm) of the tank bottom. (Adding a small foot valve will eliminate the need for repriming the pump.)

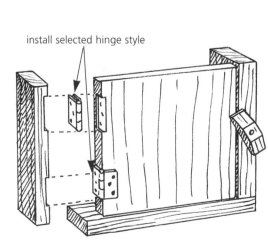

12. If you can't find a suitable nozzle, use a threaded adapter, with a pipe cap, drilled for the size hole that will produce the fountain volume and height you want. Try several caps with different size holes, but keep them all smaller than the overflow pipe.

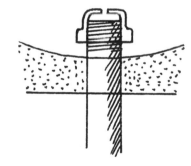

13. Extend the electric wire from the pump through the hole you left in the door frame or the mortar. Connect it to a breaker in an electric panel or use a plug-in to an outlet.

Install the door hinges, the latch, and the door itself. Fill the tank, then fill the basin, which will prime the pump. Replenish as needed.

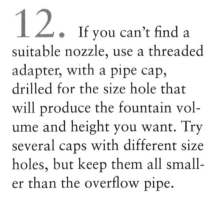

install selected hinge style

A bridge is a tribute to the stonemason's art in a way no other single structure can be. This amazing bridge was built in Scotland in the early 1800s from natural stone outcroppings over the River Moriston just before it flows into Loch Ness. Let's hope your first bridge attempt is less daunting.

CHAPTER 11

Stone Bridges

BRIDGING WATER IS ONE of stone's oldest uses. You can imagine the idea evolving from stepping-stones: Lay flat stones between steps so that water goes underneath. Or maybe a slab was laid across a narrow ditch that people kept falling into.

Until concrete and steel came into use, stone bridges were creations of permanence and utility. Graceful and beautiful, they were also sturdy. It was a stone bridge that held the wall of water in the Johnstown flood in Pennsylvania in 1889. Battered by trees, logs, railroad boxcars, and houses, it stood strong. Today, such stone bridges would cost too much to build when we have recycled beer cans and cast-off steel to use. Now you can glimpse an arched stone bridge on an abandoned country road yards away from the interstate you're speeding down. It wasn't even worth tearing down for the materials.

A simple use of stone to cross a stream is the low-water bridge, which is essentially a ford. You place stones in a shallow place in the creek in order to form a sort of pavement underwater. Theoretically, the stream flows over the stones, and they stay in place. For a while. It beats a muddy bottom you can get stuck in.

We once moved a pair of log cabins onto some property across a creek in the upper Shenandoah Valley, using an old ford. High water had deepened the creek bed, so we added stones to raise the ford and spread out the water for a shallower crossing. We were very proud of ourselves until we managed to get the truck bogged down in a soggy field before we even reached the creek.

Such crossings need periodic maintenance, of course, but they're cheap. Eventually, most people will pour a concrete slab, embedding one or more culvert pipes. When the water is low, it goes through the culverts. When it's high, it washes over the concrete. When it's really high, it eats out the soil under the ends of the slab, and sometimes sweeps the whole thing downstream.

Getting a bridge above high water means you must start the approaches high on the bank or hill slopes. Of course, when you build up the roadway, you constrict the floodplain, and the stream must squeeze between the abutments you build for the bridge. You have to line the soil with riprap or concrete to keep it from washing away. Sometimes the bridge and all will wash away anyway.

This arched cut limestone bridge has been abandoned, just a few feet off I-81 near Staunton, Virginia.

We built a covered bridge in Albemarle County, Virginia, in 1983, over a very small stream branch (see page 92). The county engineers required a survey of the drainage area to determine the effects a one-hundred-year flood would have. The result was that our bridge, over a two-foot-wide stream normally about an inch deep, had to leave an eight- by twenty-foot opening. It isn't how much water normally goes down a stream you build for, but all the hollows, draws, and valleys it drains when flash-flooded full.

Inevitably, a bridge must be built in such a way that it can span a wide area. Stone bridges had to be supported out in the water, so piers were erected in the streambed by excavating down to solid rock. Today, some ancient stone bridges are still carrying traffic. You also see piers standing in rivers with the spanning roadbeds gone, victims of high water. Midriver piers face the real hazard of waterborne trees and debris that have come off banks in storms. In nature, nothing stands forever in a waterway.

Consequently, suspension bridges were developed, allowing the entire bridge structure to be well above any high water. They're as solid as the material and engineering that go into them, just as the stone bridges were.

Simple Bridges

If you have the urge to span a stream with a delightfully artful stone bridge, start small. You might find that one-piece slab of stone to put across a trickle from a wet-weather spring. Scoop out the course of the stream to make the bridge appear more necessary.

Most common is a section of culvert pipe — metal, plastic, or concrete — with stone built up at each end to hold the path or roadway soil. Built higher, this stone retaining wall becomes the railing, too. You pour a footing under and around each end of the culvert to support the stone wall. Add a nice keystone arch across the pipe, and most people will call it a stone bridge.

A true stone bridge requires the best of the mason's art and is unbelievably complex. An alternative is a reinforced concrete arch to carry the path or roadway, with stone ends, as with the culvert. An arched form is built from footings on both sides of the stream. Rebar is laid crisscross and concrete poured to form a custom, more artistic version of the culvert. The form is taken out from underneath, and stone ends built. You gravel over the arch along with the rest of the path, and only the fish know the span is concrete.

Simple Stone Bridge

Slab stone bridge 36 in. (0.9 m) wide, 36 in. (0.9 m) long, over small stream

MATERIALS
- One stone 36 in. (0.9 m) wide, 6 in. (15 cm) or more thick, and at least 36 in. (0.9 m) long — it should be as smooth as possible, but not slick — plus several stones about 6 x 6 in. (15 x 15 cm) and up to 36 in. (0.9 m) long

TOOLS
shovel
mattock
pry bar
four-foot level
stone chisel
hammer
equipment for placing the
    stone slab

A simple stone bridge is a slab of stone laid across the stream, supported on stones at each end. These support stones are imbedded in the bank to form a level base for the slab. Necessarily, the slab must be thick and heavy to carry foot traffic. This means you'll need some help or equipment to place this stone.

1. Dig two level places 36 in. (0.9 m) long and 6 in. (15 cm) below grade on each side of the stream, parallel within 24 in. (0.6 m) of each other.

2. Lay the 6 in. (15 cm) stones on these leveled "steps" along the stream. These form the foundation for the main stone slab and should be leveled so that no wedging is necessary.

3. Lay the big stone across, and pry it into place with the bar. You will probably need a boom or tractor bucket for this job. Lacking this, you can set up a tripod of 2 x 6 (5 x 15 cm) framing lumber with a ratchet hoist to handle the big stone. The stone can be moved to the location on wooden rollers, if necessary, but should be lifted into place.

4. Once set, your simple bridge will be 6 in. (15 cm) higher than the path leading up to it. Build the path up with soil, tamp it, and add gravel to hold against erosion.

Arched Bridges

At its easiest, a true stone-arched bridge is simply a deep arch, but there's more to it than that. You could construct a series of stone arches deep enough to create a walkway over a stream, but they would be disconnected from each other. By using deeper stones alternating with shallower ones, it could all be locked together. In the finest bridge-building examples, this was done with drystone, even for vehicular traffic. I'd want to mortar it.

For a narrow bridge, ideally you'd want each arch stone to go the entire width (that's depth, if you're facing the arch). That would take advanced stone cutting, though. In the real world we do a lot of compromising, so the varied-length stones would piece their way across the width of the bridge, with nice arched faces at both ends.

We're discussing arched stone as if it were the only way to span anything wider than a trickle. It's not, but it's the only practical way to do it with stone. Laid flat to span an opening, a slab of stone must first support its own weight, then that of any traffic it carries. The tendency toward fracture is tremendous and constant. The only way to relieve this stress is to support the span in more places. That means lots of piers, a great deal of expense, and a constricted waterway.

In an arch, the weight is redirected out and down to either side of the span. The more weight, the tighter the arch. There is no fracture pressure, only compression. Stone can take a lot of compression.

A long rock wall bridges a stream with an arch.

This stone bridge at the Manassas Civil War battlefield in Virginia has used arches and buttresses to carry loads for 150 years.

A bridge arch need not be semicircular. Arches are stretched out or up to suit specific needs. For windows, they're often raised into Gothic points to let in light without removing horizontal wall mass and strength. A bridge must reach out toward the other bank, so we flatten the arch to a reasonable degree. This reduces the height and the number of arches we need.

A flat arch exerts more pressure on its bases, because leverage is at work here. Where a semicircular arch presses essentially straight down, the flattened arch pushes outward. The nearer to a flat plane, the greater the likelihood that a crushed stone or a shifting base would let the span collapse.

The shape of an arch for a bridge should derive from the load it is to carry. If your stone bridge has to support only one or two garden admirers at a time on foot, you can do just about any design you want. If you plan to support a nine-thousand-pound tractor with its wheel weights and fluid in the tires, you'll need a high arch and good footings, as well as tight stonework. Practicality would lead us back to that culvert, or at least to the formed concrete arch.

Forming for an arched bridge consists of two or more plywood arch shapes, wedged up for easy removal later. Slats are nailed from one end form to the other, with as many other plywood arches between as necessary. I'd put one every eighteen inches. A three-foot-wide bridge, to match a three-foot-wide path, would have three arch shapes of three-quarter-inch-thick plywood and a lot of three-foot pieces of one-by-four nailed on. Again, I'd mortar these stones for better holding and to avoid wedging. Mortar takes up slack nicely.

Pay attention to the end stones: They're visible. Inside stones should fit to carry the weight, but they can be ugly. Fish don't mind. You'll probably span the width with a face stone at each end eight to twelve inches deep and one center stone of a foot or more. Now and then you'll find a good stone eighteen inches deep to go halfway. If you should have one magnificent specimen three feet long with two nice ends, use it at the top as your keystone to lock everything tight.

If you like, build up the ends above the visible arch stones for a rail. Or leave the arch, then set posts and an iron or wooden rail. Gravel the path and the bridge with something subdued. I prefer round creek gravel because blue or green crushed stone looks artificial.

Certainly you should lay out the path that leads to and from the bridge so that you get a good view of it whenever possible. And again, if it spans only a trickle, even from a recirculating pump, widen a pool here and there near the bridge for proportion. A bridge needs something visual to get across. And, of course, the pool will reflect the bridge nicely.

Arched Stone Bridge

Mortared, arched stone bridge, 36 in. (0.9 cm) wide, 5 ft. (1.5 m) long

MATERIALS

- 1 ton (0.9 t) of square-cornered, uniform, workable stones, such as sandstone or limestone, about 12 in. (0.3 m) wide, 8 in. (0.2 m) thick, up to 18 in. (0.5 m) long
- Concrete: 6 sacks Portland cement, 1 ton (0.9 t) of 1 in. (2.5 cm) gravel, 1 ton (0.9 t) sand, water
- Mortar: 6 sacks Portland cement, 2 sacks lime, 2 tons (1.8 t) sand, water

- One 4 x 8 ft. (1.2 x 2.4 m) sheet of ¾ in. (2 cm) construction-grade plywood
- Two 2 x 15 in. (5 x 38 cm) boards, each 5 ft. (1.5 m) long, plus 4 wooden stakes, each 24 in. (0.6 m) long, for footing forms and braces
- 30 ft. (9 m) of 1 x 4 in. (2.5 x 10 cm) #2 yellow pine boards, plus 8D nails, for arch form braces
- Two 20 ft. (6 m) lengths of ½ in. (13 mm) rebar, safety wire

TOOLS

pick
shovel
mattock
wheelbarrow
hoe
jigsaw
claw hammer
circular saw
trowel
pointing tool
hacksaw
stone chisel
hammer

An arched stone bridge is considered by many the apex of the stonemason's craft. It ranks up there with castle turrets and freestanding stairs. You will exercise all your skill and patience on this project and take justifiable pride in its completion. When you compare yours to spans that have withstood floods, waterborne tree trunks, traffic vibration, and erosion, you will know you've arrived.

1. Because a bridge is generally built upon soft soil, a heavy footing is necessary. Dig a footing ditch, 24 in. (0.6 m) wide and 48 in. (1.2 m) long, on each side of the streambed, to below frost line or 21 in. (53 cm) down, whichever is deeper. The ditches should parallel the stream 48 in. (1.2 m) apart.

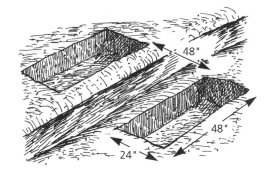

2. Mix enough concrete to fill each ditch to within 18 in. (46 cm) of the top. Start with 2 shovels of cement, 4 of sand, and 6 of gravel, plus water (see "Mixing Concrete," page 65). Mix additional batches as needed.

Cut 12 lengths of rebar, each 36 in. (0.9 m) long, and set two in the concrete of each ditch, 8 in. (21 cm) apart. Heat and bend at midpoint six lengths, forming L-shapes.

Wire three L-shapes, evenly spaced across each footing, to the two long bars. Wire another straight length of rebar near the top of the upright L-shapes in each footing.

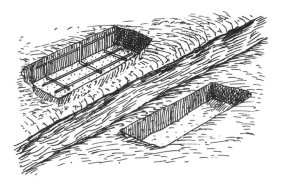

3. Pour an additional 3 in. (8 cm) of concrete over the bar. This completes the bottom of the footing.

Set a 2 x 15 in. (5 x 38 cm) board upright 12 in. (0.3 m) out from the back wall of each footing ditch. Let this board extend into slots dug in the end walls of the ditch, and brace with stakes driven diagonally into the bank. The board should rest on the bottom footing concrete.

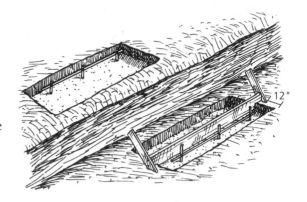

4. After the footing base has set for 10–30 minutes or more, up to an hour, pour the back, or upright wall of the footing. This concrete will bond with that previously poured, but will not force it out. If the bottom of the footing has hardened, splash water on it before pouring the back.

You now have two footings L-shaped in section, with rebar reinforcing them. Keep them wet, and let them cure for 2 days, then remove the boards.

5. Lay out and cut three arch forms from the ¾ in. (2 cm) plywood. These should follow a curve coming up 12 in. (31 cm) to an apex in 4 ft. (1.2 m), or half the height of a semicircle. In other words, the center of the curve should be 12 in. (31 cm) higher than the ends of the form.

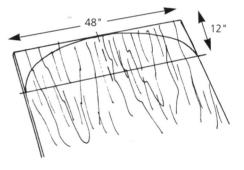

6. Set these three arches up on edge 24 in. (0.6 m) apart and nail a 1 x 4 in. (2.5 x 10 cm) board every 4 in. (10 cm) across the outside edges, tying the three arches together. Set this 48 x 48 in. (1.2 x 1.2 m) form between the concrete footings, and wedge it in place. (You'll remove the wedges to get the form out after the bridge is built.)

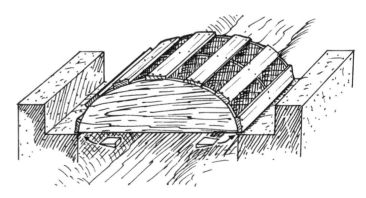

7. To mix mortar, begin with 9 shovels of sand, 2 of cement, and 1 of lime, plus water (see "Mixing Mortar for Stonework," page 71).

Begin laying stone up against the vertical wall of the L-shaped footing. Shape or find stones with a taper in their thicknesses, so that from the up- and downstream sides of the bridge, the joints between stones radiate from a central point.

Use well-shaped stones for the upstream and downstream sides of the arch. These should be of varying lengths across the form so that joints do not run. Fill stones, which will be below the finished surface of the bridge walkway, can be quite rough, since they're hidden. Use as much mortar as necessary with these interior stones, but keep *visible* joints tight, approximately ½ to 1 in. (1.3 to 2.5 cm).

Lay stones up from both footings, all across the arched form, mortaring smoothly on top, and keeping radial end joints in line. Lay the stone in such a way that if the mortar were to disintegrate, the taper of the stones would hold the stones of the arch in place.

8. Lay an impressive keystone at each apex on the upstream and downstream sides of the form, and fill between with other keystone-shaped stones. All the face stones (those that are visible) should be the full height for strength, but those inside can be thinner — you can use two or more to obtain the necessary height up to the top of the footing (the pathway surface height), since the horizontal joints won't weaken the structure.

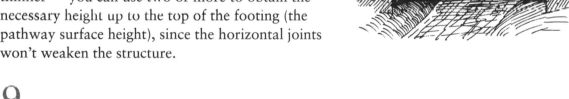

9. After 2 days — during which you must keep the stonework wet — pull the wedges out and remove the form.

The L-shaped footings hold against settling and also against end thrust. If the arch were semicircular, pressure would be down only. With this elongated span, there is outward thrust, too. The footing, thick and reinforced, will hold this both ways.

You can build perpendicular walls up from the ends of the arch if you wish. This can be done before or after the form is removed. Build the path to the bridge up with soil, tamp, and put down gravel to hold against erosion.

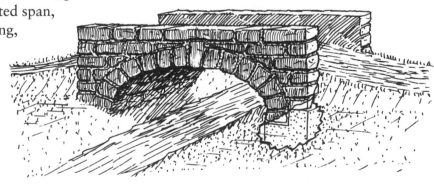

Stone veneer between load-bearing beams combines with the antique heart pine of the staircase and chinked log walls to create one of the most interesting corners in the McRaven house.

CHAPTER 12

Stone in Interior Spaces

STONEWORK INSIDE A HOUSE is a wonderful feature. Although usually associated with fireplace facades, it also has other historical applications. House walls in such treeless regions as northern Scotland and above the timberline in Switzerland were often all stone. In England, the timber frames were often filled with stone.

Today's heated houses mean interior stone should have insulation and a vapor barrier between it and the great outdoors. Without these materials, moisture builds up and heat flows through. Builders sometimes use stone to fill between timbers for inside walls, but it's a veneer over insulation. Our kitchen addition is timber frame, with some of the spaces between in stone and some in stucco. All stone would be too dark and too much the same. The stucco gives a visual break and, painted off-white, lightens the room and accents the timbers.

Some entire interior walls are stone. Fireplaces are often set in all-stone walls, sometimes with raised stone hearths. Stone is a good interior wall covering, requires no maintenance, but, of course, the labor involved is high. As with all stonework, however, its value far exceeds its cost.

Veneer Walls

Interior stonework just about always means it is veneer, maybe four inches thick, which imposes some limitations in style. The currently popular dry-stack look is very difficult as thin veneer, simply because there isn't much depth for the mortar — all out of sight — to hold. Dry-stack is easier and stronger if it is deeper and the mortar has more to hold onto.

A visible mortar joint is obviously stronger here, since stones are bonded all around their edges. A stone stuck to a wall with just the backing mortar is not very secure. Carefully done, a thin mortar joint of one-half inch or less that is struck deeply is still attractive. Any interior stonework gets closer scrutiny than outside work and should be neat.

The demands made by interior work make it slower going, too. If I'm laying up twenty square feet of veneer on the outside of a wall, that gets reduced to maybe ten square feet inside between beams. Not only are there constant edges against the wood, but there may also be angles created by diagonal bracing. And there must be a lot of masonry ties in situations like this, preferably one for each stone.

Masonry ties are corrugated metal strips nailed or screwed into the structural wall. If this wall is sheathed in plywood or fiberboard, such as Celotex, anchor the ties at the studs and fire-stop crosspieces. The fewer the number of ties, the weaker the stonework, especially if it is thin or has very narrow joints.

Interior stonework can be painstaking. It requires tight mortar joints and considerable shaping, especially where stone meets wood. An insulating wall is sandwiched between the interior stone and the exterior stone to form a twelve-inch-thick wall. The interior stone wall stays room temperature and never sweats.

Veneer stonework constitutes most of the stone masonry practiced today. Of the forty or so masons I know, only three or four routinely do solid stonework. The demand is for veneered concrete block basements, chimneys, walls instead of solid work.

Veneer work means, of course, using stones the maximum interior wall thickness or less. Thin stones must be packed behind with mortar. Let this set up at least a day before laying more on top, or the stone above will push the thin one out as it settles into the mortar.

It is often a good idea to "butter" the backs of veneer with mortar to ensure the mortar's bonding to the stone. I spread mortar on both the stone surface and the surface to be veneered and then fill between with mortar for a good bond.

Don't use freshly quarried stone inside. The new, raw look won't weather and never looks quite right. Some lichens on fieldstone will live for years indoors if near sunlight from a window and if watered regularly. I always enjoy splashing water on lichens and seeing how quickly their color brightens. Remember that most house interiors are much drier than the outside air, especially in winter heat.

The Sowell House museum restoration at Michie Tavern in Virginia includes a kitchen in the drystone basement. Stonework of this kind can be effectively adapted for the modern home.

Veneer Wall

Stone veneer 6 in. (15 cm) thick over a concrete block wall 8 ft. (2.4 m) high and 20 ft. (6 m) long

MATERIALS
- 5 tons (4.5 t) stone up to 6 in. (15 cm) thick with as many long stones as possible, with parallel tops and bottoms
- Mortar: 6 bags Portland cement, 2 sacks lime, 2 tons (1.8 t) sand, water
- Corrugated masonry ties

TOOLS
shovel
wheelbarrow
hoe
trowel
pointing tool
stone chisel
hammer
wire brush

Veneer over concrete blocks is common. Usually a block mason installs galvanized masonry ties to the wall at random, and you'll be able to use some of these for your stonework pattern. Other ties will just be in the way, but you can bend them aside. Don't leave an expanse of 24 in. (0.6) square or so without a tie. If no tie is in the right place for you, use a hardened masonry nail to set one where you need it — just above a stone. Be sure to seal the mortar joint tightly at the top of the veneer wall so water can't get inside and freeze, or all the masonry ties in the world won't hold the stones to the wall.

1. To mix mortar, begin with 9 shovels of sand, 2 of cement, and 1 of lime, plus water (see "Mixing Mortar for Stonework," page 71).

A concrete block or poured concrete wall will be set on a wide footing. Begin laying stone on this footing in a ledge pattern for strength. You may use as many random shapes as you like, but always return to the horizontal ledge pattern.

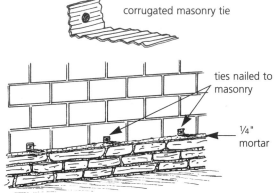

corrugated masonry tie

2. Utilize masonry ties that the block mason will have set in the block joints. If none are provided, you can set them as needed using short, hard masonry nails or an explosive-charge tool. Get a tie in over every other stone in every course. Put ¼ in. (6 mm) of mortar on top of the stone, then bend the masonry tie into place on it.

ties nailed to masonry

¼" mortar

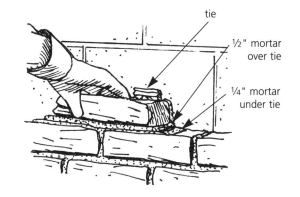

tie

½" mortar over tie

¼" mortar under tie

3. Put another ½ in. (13 mm) of mortar over the tie. Set the next stone over this. The corrugations of the metal tie, sandwiched between the stones, will hold them to the block wall. Because the stone will settle, the finished joints will be about ½ in. (13 mm).

4. In setting veneer stones, "butter" the backs of the stones and also the surface of the block wall to ensure a bond. Press each stone into place, fill any voids with mortar, and pack with the pointing tool. Since all the stones won't be an ideal 6 in. (15 cm) thick, fill behind shallow ones with mortar. Keep the wall wet for 2 days.

If you want to veneer over a frame wall, set masonry ties as needed into the studs with nails or screws. Locate the studs behind the fiberboard or plywood, marking with a chalk line so you'll know where to set the ties. Set a tie wherever you need it along the vertical line.

A frame wall will give no bonding to the stone at all, unlike a concrete or concrete block wall. This means you'll need more masonry ties, so put one in each stud over each stone. The rest of the veneering techniques are the same as for a concrete block wall.

Stone veneer will cover the exterior of this post-and-beam framework to create a beautiful entrance for an "English basement". The veneer covers an insulated frame wall between the posts.

Hearths

Stone is often used for hearths, whether the design is raised or flush with the floor. There is still a firm belief among many masons that the floor-level fireplace gives more heat than the raised one. That has not been my experience, however.

Generally a masonry support of concrete block is brought up to carry the weight of the hearth. Flagstone is used for the hearth itself, often extended an inch or two over the edge for raised hearths. Here I like round-edged creekstones, particularly where there are young children. Raised hearths are usually about sixteen inches high, and a fall against the sharp corner of one can hurt the child and traumatize the parents.

Raised hearths are a modern adaptation, very nice to sit on or to prop your feet on. When fireplaces were used for cooking, raising the hearth would have saved many a frontier woman's back. My wife figures that the early mason didn't build a raised hearth because he didn't do the cooking.

The fact is, our ancestors, particularly the English, Irish, and Scots, feared fire. The firepit and open smoke hole of the Middle Ages were replaced grudgingly with the chimney by the sixteenth century, but it was completely outside the house wall.

The four-foot millstone hearth for this fireplace is a combination of the local greenstone and a granite.

Bigger, more expensive houses kept the kitchen out back in a separate (and, we imagine, expendable) building. The American frontier house developed largely with those dangerous chimneys outside and the hearth down at floor level.

German masons put the fireplace and chimney in the middle of the cabin, where they would do the most good. The heat that flowed out through the stones of the Scotch-Irish cottage stayed in the German house. The Scandinavians put the fireplace out of the way in the corner, but still inside.

Eventually masonry heaters were developed, which absorb much of the heat on its way up the chimney to radiate it into the house. Baffles and a circuitous route for the smoke extract what would be wasted heat. These are also called Russian or Finnish fireplaces, and I am currently building one in our house. For more about building fireplaces, see my book *Building with Stone* (Pownal, Vt.: Storey Communications, Garden Way Publishing, 1989).

Stone Floors

Entryway floors are frequently made of flagstone or slate, which helps bring the feel of the outside indoors. If the flagstone is thick, the framing joists must be lower. If you use half-inch-thick slate, it can be set in mortar to equal the height of the finished floor.

Additional support for a framed floor really is not necessary if the framing conforms to the building codes. A layer of slate as an entryway doesn't weigh any more than a hefty piece of furniture or large people standing close together. Modern buildings are overframed so floors and ceilings won't flex and crack drywall or make occupants uneasy.

If really thick, heavy stone is to be used, joists underneath can be doubled, or "sistered." If reinforcing steel wire or mesh, such as metal lath, is used in the layer of mortar under the stone, however, the weight will be spread out, and no flexing or cracking should occur.

Setting stone on a wooden subfloor is always a bit of a gamble. I like to set the stone in a bed of mortar strengthened with reinforcing wire. The mortar should be poured over sheet plastic to seal it away from the subfloor.

Entire rooms can be floored in stone in this manner. I prefer to set stone floors in mortar on a concrete slab, because wood moves with moisture changes and that can cause cracks in the masonry. Another, cheaper method is to set the stone on fine gravel with no slab underneath it. The gravel should have a plastic vapor barrier under it, and so should the concrete slab. In any stone floor application, grout the joints with mortar to help hold the stones in place.

Some masons grout the stone joints in floors, patios, or paths by using a dry mortar mix, then misting it with water. That works, but don't leave the "dry" mix more than an hour or two before you wet it, or the moisture present in the sand will activate the cement before you have finished, and it will crumble and weather away later.

This patio floor of rounded stone sits on a gravel bed. Mortar will fill the joints.

Hearth and Stone Floor

A stone hearth or floor, 2 x 5 ft. (0.6 x 1.5 m) over a concrete subfloor slab

MATERIALS

- Flagstone to cover 2 x 5 ft. (0.6 x 1.5 m) for the hearth, or proportionate quantities for larger floors. Stones should be 2 in. (5 cm) maximum thickness, in random shapes
- Mortar: 1 sack Portland cement, ⅓ sack lime, 300 lb. (140 kg) sand, water

TOOLS

circular saw
masonry blades
shovel
wheelbarrow
hoe
trowel
wire brush
pointing tool
four-foot level
stone chisel
striking and rubber hammers

A stone floor and a hearth are identical except for size. Techniques are the same; materials, the same. One difference: Over a framed wooden floor, where hearths and entryway stone is usually at the edge of a room, an entire floor will extend to the center of the joist span. Here is the weakest point of the floor, and flexing, if any, will occur here. Where possible, it's a good idea to support the center of the joists with a girder underneath, itself supported by piers.

1. Dry-fit the hearth or a section of floor by shaping where necessary. Leave about 1 in. (2.5 cm) between flagstones. Shape corners and cut straight lines by scoring ⅛ in. (3 mm) deep at a pass with the circular saw and a masonry blade. Do this outdoors and upwind because of the heavy dust the procedure creates. Cut about ¼ in. (6 mm) deep on both sides, then break the stone with the hammer, using a piece of wood to cushion the blow.

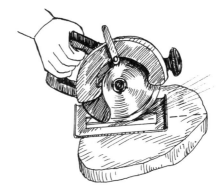

2. To mix mortar, begin with 9 shovels of sand, 2 of cement, and 1 of lime, plus water (see "Mixing Mortar for Stonework," page 71). Lay ½ in. (13 mm) or so of mortar on the concrete subfloor to bed the stones in. Build up more for thinner stones. Then set the stones, leveling as you go.

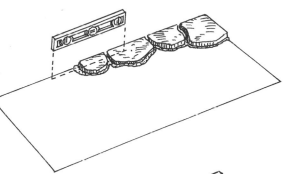

3. Use the level carefully on a large floor; the tendency is to let portions of it come up too high or go too low. Many masons check their "flat work" with a long 2 x 6 in. (5 x 15 cm) timber up on edge to detect irregularities. A high stone can be bumped down with the rubber hammer. One that is too low must be removed and more mortar added under it.

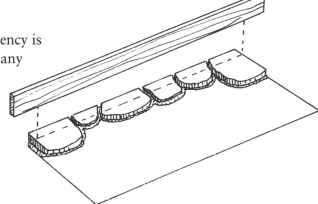

4. Grout between stones with mortar and level it smooth. After about 2 hours, you can clean up with a wet sponge, which will also smooth the surface of the mortar. Keep moist for 2 days.

Seal a stone hearth or floor with two coats of masonry sealer a week after it has been laid. This will prevent erosion of the mortar joints and will bring out colors in the stone. Two brands commonly used are Drylock and Thompson's.

APPENDIX

Frost-Line Zones

The map below indicates the maximum depth in inches that frost penetrates for each region shown. These are general recommendations only. Consult your local records for more specific guidance for your area.

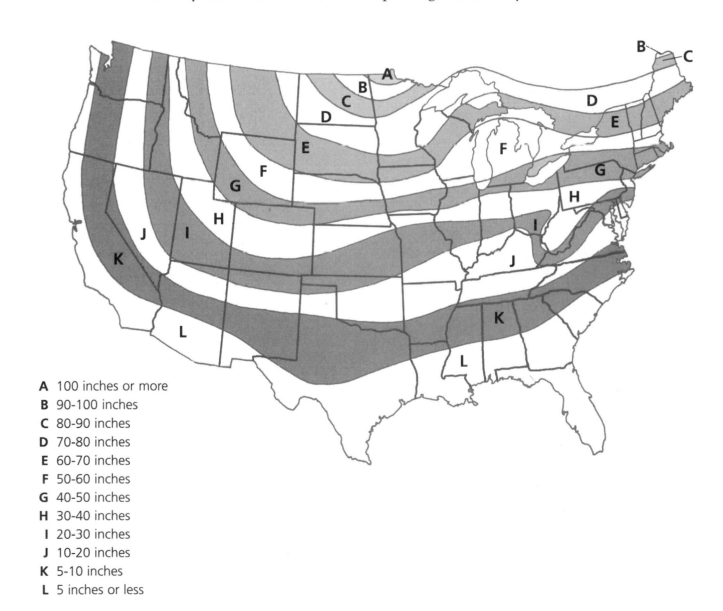

A 100 inches or more
B 90-100 inches
C 80-90 inches
D 70-80 inches
E 60-70 inches
F 50-60 inches
G 40-50 inches
H 30-40 inches
I 20-30 inches
J 10-20 inches
K 5-10 inches
L 5 inches or less

Glossary

angle-iron rack	Framework used in pickup truck to haul ladders and long lumber.
ashlar	Angled patterns in straight lines of stonework.
basalt	A hard stone difficult to shape.
bead	A jutting horizontal protrusion near the top of a chimney or decorative pillar.
capstone	Stone on top of a wall.
come-along	Ratchet hand winch.
corbeling	Steps out from a wall to support a cantilevered structure.
creekstone	Smooth, rounded quartzite stone worn by water.
crowbar	Curved pry bar normally used for demolition.
dress	To shape a stone finely to fit a space.
dry-stack	Stonework with mortar recessed so that it is invisible.
drystone	Stonework with no mortar.
eyebolt	Bolt with a loop in it for attaching hardware.
feather	Metal spacer used with wedges in drilled holes to crack apart stone.
feldspar	One of the crystalline minerals in granite.
fieldstone	Stone picked up from the surface of the ground.
filter fabric	Material used to hold soil against erosion.
glue-on stones	Thin stones stuck on a surface with mortar.
gneiss	Hard, metamorphic rock, not easily worked.
granite	Hardest of the normally worked stone; porous, good for lichens and moss to grow on.
greenstone	An irregularly shaped igneous stone common to Maryland and Virginia.

igneous	Fire-made stone.
keystone	The top stone in an arch, or the center stone in a flat span.
ledgestone	Pattern of stonework utilizing horizontal joints.
limestone	Sedimentary rock, easily worked; usually gray, highly favored by masons.
lintel	Stone spanning an opening.
maul	Heavy, edged hammer for splitting.
metamorphic	Stone changed by heat or compression.
mica	Mineral that occurs in thin sheets; bits of it sparkle.
pier	Vertical stone column that supports structures.
pintle	A hinge pin that sets into stonework.
pry bar	Any tool used to lever stones or other heavy objects.
quartz	Any crystalline stone.
quartzite	Sandstone, usually a harder, denser type.
quoin	Stone extending from corner, usually thicker than the wall.
radial edges	The sloped edges of stones in an arch that lead to a common point.
raking	Removing excess mortar from between stones.
riprap	Irregular stone used for fill or to hold against erosion.
running joint	Vertical joints that are aligned.
Russian fireplace	Masonry heater with baffles to retain heat.
sandstone	Sedimentary rock made up of compressed sand.
schist	A metamorphic crystalline rock, easy to split into planes.
sedimentary	Stone formed by minerals settled as sediment, then compressed.
shale	Thinly layered soft stone.
shim	Small, spacer stone used to fill a gap or to prop a larger stone.
"shot" stone	Stone quarried with explosives.
snap ties	Metal ties that hold concrete forms in place.
slate	Sedimentary rock in layers, used for roofs and floors.

snatch block	Pulley used with cable or rope to increase pulling power.
soapstone	Soft stone that resists heat well.
star drill	Chisel-like drill struck with a hammer to make holes in rock.
step bulkheads	Boards set across a sloping ditch to hold poured concrete so that the surface of the concrete will be level.
stone point	Sharp, pointed chisel for finishing stone faces.
tie-stone	Long stone that extends across a wall.
true up	To make level or plumb.
wedges	Stone chips for leveling; metal tools for splitting stone.
zigzag pintle	The part of a hinge pin that extends into stonework mortar and holds it in place.

Index

Other Storey Titles You Will Enjoy

Building with Stone, by Charles McRaven. An introduction to the art and craft of creating stone structures. Includes detailed step-by-step instructions and information on tools for stonework and acquiring stone. More than 200 photos. 192 pages. Paperback. ISBN #0-88266-550-2.

Building Stone Walls, by John Vivian. A thorough reference book including information on equipment requirements, instructions for creating wall foundations, coping with drainage problems, and hints for incorporating gates, fences, and stiles. 112 pages. Paperback. ISBN #0-88266-074-8.

Step-by-Step Outdoor Stonework: Over Twenty Easy-to-Build Projects for Your Patio and Garden, Edited by Mike Lawrence. Includes complete information on estimating costs and quantities, information on tools, materials, and site preparation. 96 pages. Paperback. ISBN #0-88266-891-9.

Build Your Own Stone House: Using the Easy Slipform Method, by Karl and Sue Schwenke. Features complete instructions on tools, types of materials, estimating needed amounts, siting the house, and excavating. Includes information on using and removing forms. 176 pages. Paperback. ISBN #0-88266-639-8.

Stonescaping: A Guide to Using Stone in Your Garden, by Jan Kowalczewski Whitner. Thirty color photos help to show you how to incorporate stone into many garden features, including paths, steps, walls, ponds, and rock gardens. Includes twenty basic designs. 168 pages. Hardcover. ISBN #0-88266-755-6. Paperback. ISBN #0-88266-756-4.

How to Build Small Barns & Outbuildings, by Monte Burch. Complete plans and step-by-step instructions for 20 projects. Includes 70 photos and 150 line drawings for illustration and reference. 288 pages. Hardcover. ISBN #0-88266-774-2. Paperback. ISBN #0-88266-773-4.

Fences for Pasture and Garden, by Gail Damerow. The complete guide to choosing, planning, and building today's best fences: wire, rail, electric, high-tension, temporary, woven, and snow. Also features chapters on gates and trellises. 160 pages. Hardcover. ISBN #0-88266-754-8. Paperback. ISBN #0-88266-753-X.

Timber Frame Construction: All About Post-and-Beam Building, by Jack Sobon and Roger Schroeder. Explains the basics of timber-frame construction in terms the beginner can understand. Includes information on framing, designing for strength and beauty, using modern tools, and selecting the appropriate wood. 208 pages. Paperback. ISBN #0-88266-365-8.

Building Small Barns, Sheds & Shelters, by Monte Burch. Covers tools, materials, foundations, framing, sheathing, wiring, plumbing, and finish work for barns, woodsheds, garages, fencing, and animal housing. Includes detailed line drawings and photos. 256 pages. Paperback. ISBN #0-88266-245-7.

Reviving Old Houses, by Alan Dan Orme. Practical advice on roofs, walls, masonry, glazing, insulation, plumbing, doors, stairs, floors, exteriors, and more. 180 pages. Hardcover. ISBN #0-88266-582-0. Paperback. ISBN #0-88266-563-4.

Low-Cost Pole Building Construction, by Ralph Wolfe. Includes ten building plans with elevation drawings and materials lists, 19 examples of already-built homes, and detailed description of pole building construction. 192 pages. Paperback. ISBN #0-88266-170-1.

These books and other Storey books are available at your bookstore, farm store, garden center, or directly from Storey Publishing, Schoolhouse Road, Pownal, Vermont 05261, or by calling 800-441-5700. www.storey.com